Managerial Communication and the Brain

Managerial Communication and the Brain

Applying Neuroscience to Leadership Practices

Dirk Remley

 BUSINESS EXPERT PRESS

Managerial Communication and the Brain: Applying Neuroscience to Leadership Practices

Copyright © Business Expert Press, LLC, 2017.

First published in 2017 by
Business Expert Press, LLC
222 East 46th Street, New York, NY 10017
www.businessexpertpress.com

ISBN-13: 978-1-63157-936-3 (paperback)
ISBN-13: 978-1-63157-937-0 (e-book)

Business Expert Press Corporate Communication Collection

Collection ISSN: 2156-8162 (print)
Collection ISSN: 2156-8170 (electronic)

Cover and interior design by Exeter Premedia Services Private Ltd., Chennai, India

First edition: 2017

10 9 8 7 6 5 4 3 2 1

Printed in the United States of America.

Abstract

This book takes a neuroscientific approach to explaining elements of effective managerial and leadership communication in a concise way. These include communicating with various audiences and in a variety of situations managers and leaders face regularly.

The book includes an easy-to-use guide to help the reader apply this understanding of neuroscience to principles of rhetoric toward developing effective messages. Several specific examples, including detailed explanations of them, illustrate applications. Drawn from real situations, activities, and cases, also, encourage practice and facilitate immediate application to situations the reader may be experiencing.

Encouraging principles of lean processes, especially lean communication, the book will benefit any in a position of leadership no matter the size of the team or organization, or the professional setting—business, health care, technology, manufacturing, and others. It will also benefit those training for such positions—graduate business and management students and those in leadership development programs.

Keywords

executive communication, leadership communication, lean communication, managerial communication, neuroscience and leadership communication, persuasion and leadership, persuasion and management

Contents

Acknowledgments

I thank my editor, Dr Debbie DuFrene, for her patience, feedback, and detailed style editing of each chapter. I also thank Dr Marion Philadelphia of the University of Southern California and Dr Dorothy McCawley of the University of Florida for their comments and feedback.

Of course, I thank my wife and family for their unwavering support and patience.

CHAPTER 1

Introduction

In any organization, management—from bottom to top—is concerned with efficiency. In business writing courses, a desired outcome of the course is that students learn to phrase messages concisely; indeed, conciseness is one of the concepts of business writing that is paramount to the nature of business communication. Assignments in such courses frequently include a word or page limit to encourage students to practice skills related to clarity and conciseness. In business, a desired outcome is profit; one of the primary measures of performance is net profit in a given period. In manufacturing, a valued outcome is that production takes less than a certain amount of time without quality being compromised. In most offices, a goal is to perform tasks using a certain amount of effort and in a given period of time.

Let's consider a situation in which you are the manager of an employee who has conveyed concern about his performance review, which indicated a lack of efficiency as a main issue. Though there is evidence that the employee's work could have been done more efficiently without compromising quality, the employee explains that he would not have felt comfortable using the more efficient approach and that his approach is better. In challenging you to explain why you had mentioned the efficiency issue on the report, the employee acknowledges that he knew there was another way to do the jobs but understands that good leaders "break the rules" to get the best results possible. Indeed, in an effort to show their leadership potential, this employee acknowledges that he "often" break the rules, even if it means violating instructions given by management.

While you could respond merely with the statement that he violated the explicitly stated standard of efficiency and leave it at that, you do not. Clearly, the employee aspires to a position of leadership and has some experience with leadership development. The employee would not respond favorably to that blunt message; in this case, "respond favorably" means that the employee would have respected the response and learned from it. Instead, you acknowledge what the employee learned in his own leadership training experience (breaking rules) as well as what you learned in your own management and leadership training: be careful in breaking rules, don't set out to break the rules all the time, and don't break a rule directly connected to the desired outcome. Further, you implicitly use some elements of neuroscience that you understand could elicit a more favorable response.

Though your response is relatively long, the employee responds favorably. He acknowledges his appreciation for the detailed response and, also, acknowledges his appreciation for the links you made to leadership concepts. By the end of this chapter, you will understand several reasons why the message was successful. By the end of the book, you will understand how to apply the neuroscientific concepts involved in a variety of situations.

Topics and Goals of This Book

Communication is a primary tool of management and leadership, affecting every part of business. While management and leadership involve several different attributes to distinguish one from the other, as Jacob Morgan notes, "managers must be leaders."[1] Ideas are conveyed through communication to an audience; and the audience assesses how to respond to the idea, based on how it is communicated. The audience is the center of the message; not the end. Managers at all levels of an organization need to think carefully about how to phrase a message in order to get the best desired response. The higher up one goes in management—to executive levels and other leadership positions—the more challenging these messages become, because they often deal with elements of changing behaviors or structure and affect many people.

Whether presented in written or oral form, a proposal that does not motivate the audience to the desired action will not be accepted. A message informing an audience of an accounting or financial issue will not be understood if the sender does not consider the audience's background with accounting and finance. A directive related to changing a policy or procedure will not be well received if it does not address the audience's concerns and fears about change. Training material that does not address the audience's learning style and cognitive needs will not be effective.

An understanding of things that affect an audience's perception of a message and understanding of it will enable the communicator to convey the message most effectively. This point is not new to anyone who manages others. Anyone educated in principles of management has learned that management is more a social science and art form than anything else. Management involves leadership of varying degrees, and leadership involves managing people; a manager at any level is trying to help the people she leads do their jobs well by keeping them motivated and helping them understand their job expectations. Even communication between managers at different levels requires similar dynamics of audience analysis in order to be effective.

Peter Drucker called management a liberal art because management at any level involves being able to think critically about a situation or context, analyze options available to solve a problem with that situation, and communicate decisions effectively.[2] Aristotle labeled rhetoric as an art rather than a science; however, he also pointed out that rhetoric is affected by the audience's biological makeup.[3] Indeed, social sciences are part of liberal arts, and social interactions affect biological development. Interestingly, articles have appeared in The *Harvard Business Review* that reinforce this blending between art and science relative to communication.[4, 5] Scholarship in cognitive neuroscience is helping people in various decision making and leadership positions understand why the way certain messages are presented causes a certain response from an audience. That is why it is important to consider neuroscientific attributes that are involved in various messages, particularly messages common to managers and leaders: persuasive messages, informational messages, and instructional messages. The goal of this book is to help you understand these attributes and develop effective messages that can be conveyed either in writing or orally.

This book includes information about various forms of managerial and leadership-related communication, especially written communication such as correspondence and short reports. While it includes some principles of oral communication, there are subtle differences between a written proposal and one presented orally; in many cases, a proposal may be delivered using both—a written report and an oral presentation. Consequently, this book includes many of the same kinds of business writing topics covered in most business writing textbooks or handbooks. However, this book differs from those in that it emphasizes neuroscientific concepts to explain approaches to responding to particular managerial or leadership-related communication situations.

While other textbooks or handbooks provide tips on how to make a message effective, applying reader (or "you") perspective, for example, I show how an understanding of certain concepts of neuroscience can help improve a message's effectiveness and get desired results. As with many textbooks, this book emphasizes the relationship of audience and purpose within a message. However, the neuroscientific approach helps to explain why certain messages work better than others relative to audience and purpose. How do I know that this understanding can accomplish desired results? I have used my own application of the concepts in various management or leadership situations resulting in desired outcomes. A number of these are included in this book as examples and cases. Most of them address what Hamm labeled "The Five Messages Leaders Must Manage" in a May 2006 *Harvard Business Review* article.[6]

Hamm identifies five particular messages, or situations, requiring careful approaches to addressing them, which I extend to the general nature of the situation. Some of my extensions are very close to, if not the same as, Hamm's original characterization of his terms. I list each of Hamm's terms, a general description of it, and my extension:

- Organizational Hierarchy—organizational restructuring (communication about change),
- Financial results—how one defines "results" and communicates about results (communication about performance),
- Your Job—how the leader represents his or her role to him or herself and others (communicating parameters of your job),
- Time Management—communicating one's perception of efficient use of time (how to use time efficiently), and
- Corporate Culture—clearly defining the organization's values and how to meet them toward understanding links between individual success and organizational success (identifying organizational goals and ways individuals can meet them successfully, creating a clear understanding of culture).

Throughout the book, we will consider scholarship in rhetoric, neuroscience, and managerial communication. I describe applications of theory to practice and link certain practices to theory. As such, this book combines scholarly theory with proven application. A background in the theories that drive effective practice is important to understand why a given practice works and to facilitate transference of the practical skill to similar situations. Most of the theoretical review is integrated into the first few chapters, with each subsequent chapter integrating less theory and more practical application. All chapters include examples of the application of related skills. Several include activities to provide you with practice. This chapter also provides some basic information about concepts of rhetoric and neuroscience relevant to managerial communication.

Chapter 2 covers concepts and their relationship to principles of communication and rhetoric that you may already understand. However, those who are already familiar with these concepts will benefit as well from the explanations. I provide an overview of some principles of the different forms of business writing covered in those other textbooks and handbooks, linking neuroscience to those principles. Because of the concise approach to this book, I do not detail those concepts as they may be covered in other textbooks. You may view more information and examples of the various kinds of communication by searching websites using the concept as a search term. The book avoids technical, scientific jargon; so, you do not need an advanced understanding of rhetoric or neuroscience to benefit from this book.

Chapters 3 through eight cover specific examples of messages I have used in different situations, mostly in leadership situations—corresponding from a leadership position or to leadership. For 4 years I have coordinated the business writing course required of all undergraduate business majors at my institution. This coordination includes mentoring and directing six to seven teachers in any given semester. As such, I lead this group, which usually changes from semester to semester. My role as coordinator also has involved acting as a liaison between the Department of English and the College of Business, communicating with leadership of that college and reporting to leadership in my department; I have communicated with different levels of leadership. I have had several opportunities in these settings to practice what is discussed in this book. However, a couple of the examples fall outside of that context, yet involve communicating with leadership. I have applied these concepts in communications with company leadership in my position as a customer, for example. You also will see the concepts applied in business-to-business settings.

Each chapter includes a scenario for you to consider and decide how you might approach it. This activity hopefully will encourage critical thinking about the concepts and how to use them to create an effective message in response to a problem posed in a given situation.

I cannot guarantee the success of your own application of the concepts to your situation; a message that moves one person may not move another. Much depends on the audience's disposition. Again, while science is involved, much makes communication an art form.

Why Is It Important to Consider Neuroscience within Managerial and Leadership Communication?

People are affected by their cultural upbringing, and this influence is manifested in one's neurons. Neurons are part of your brain; they help facilitate connections between parts of the brain involved in perception, cognition, and decision making. Your fears, values, and perceptions of the world evolve through social interactions that affect biological phenomena associated with neurons. Indeed, the social experience affects the biological development.

The purpose of a message and its audience are intertwined. A message must consider the audience's disposition to be most effective. This is echoed not only in scholarship related to rhetoric but in leadership and executive-oriented articles as well, as observed with the several references to articles published in business-related journals including the *Harvard Business Review*. The smaller the audience, the more able one is to meet that task. However, if a large group of people is involved as an audience and you can ascertain that the people in that group share common attributes such as values or experiences, a message should make an appeal to those common elements.

This book focuses on messages addressed to relatively small audiences—not much more than a handful of people. Consequently, it allows for a better understanding of the audience's disposition than attempting to understand the disposition of each person in a larger audience—10 or more, for example. This disposition may be relative to social disposition or biological or physical disposition. Aristotle notes that this disposition likely involves an audience that may have "limited intellectual scope and limited capacity to follow an extended chain of reasoning."[7] Drucker observes that management, "is deeply embedded in culture."[8] So, social disposition is just as important as physical disposition. An audience's general attitude toward their work also is an important consideration.

Managers learn about McGregor's (1960) management theories—"Theory X" and "Theory Y" management styles.[9] These styles are relative to employee attitude about work. Very broadly, Theory X characterizes employees as not liking work, preferring to be directed, and motivated by job security or the threat of losing their job. The Theory X management style requires management to be authoritarian. Theory Y characterizes employees as motivated to work, wanting to exercise independent thinking skills and creativity, and willing to exceed expectations if they recognize a reasonable reward is offered. The Theory Y management style encourages management to offer employees latitude for creative thinking and flexibility to define their responsibilities, understanding that the employee wants responsibility.

I would argue that the X/Y philosophy is not an "either/or" binary distinction; it should be represented as a spectrum or line, with "Heavily Theory X" (requiring considerable supervision or direction and having very little motivation beyond the minimum required to keep their job) at one end and "Heavily Theory Y" (having strong independent and creative thinking skills, ambitious, desiring more responsibilities) at the other end. Each employee exists somewhere along that spectrum, and each requires a different message to encourage them to do a given task. For some, getting the boss's approval is enough reward, knowing it means they will keep their job. For some others, that approval may be recognized as a "notch" toward helping them get a promotion or salary increase. For still others, the reward must be acknowledged prior to their being motivated to do the task itself. Each one falls at a different point along that X/Y spectrum.

A message must be conveyed in a way that suits the audience's background, perceptions of the world, motivations, and practices—according to their capacity for cognition.

Scholarship in rhetoric draws on studies from the social science and humanities disciplines of cognitive neuroscience—social psychology, for example. Rhetoric is certainly a social dynamic, as it attempts to facilitate a desired response from an audience. Scholarship in neuroscience helps to explain scientifically some of the findings reported in scholarship in rhetoric.

Scholarship in cognitive neuroscience involves five general disciplines: cognitive psychology, philosophy, linguistics, biology, and chemistry. These represent a cross among humanities and scientific fields. The field of cognitive neuroscience devotes much attention to understanding how one processes information toward cognition.

Humanities scholars tend to examine how language and social interactions affect our understanding of the world. Indeed, Hutchins[10] and Pinker[11] for example, describe cognition as a series of developmental processes affected by historical dynamics as well as previous social experiences related to certain tasks. In each case, research in cognitive neuroscience has found that cognition is a multisensory process. Multiple senses are involved in any social interaction—visual, aural, and spatial orientation, as well as gesture, touch, and smell, depending on the environment in which the interaction occurs. Likewise, language is generally recognized as being aural or oral or visual—print-linguistic text is a visual representation.

This appreciation of the senses is important, because *it may be better to communicate directly with someone in person than via e-mail,* for example. Meaning and effect can be lost or misunderstood when conveyed only in writing. An in-person meeting will eliminate a lot of potential confusion. It also may have a more powerful effect than writing because of neuroscience-related dynamics. Again, most of this book pertains to written communication, but I allude a few times to situations when an in-person meeting will be more effective than an e-mail message. One may, for example, compose a script of the message prior to a meeting or presentation, using that phrasing in an in-person meeting that integrates other visual and auditory cues to enhance the effect of the message.

A number of visual dynamics come into play with an in-person meeting (e.g., color of dress, facial expressions, smell of cologne or perfume, posture, and even a handshake), and I discuss some of these dynamics in this book.

Cognitive Neuroscience and Managerial and Leadership Communication

This chapter includes an overview of several concepts related to neuroscience and rhetoric as applied to managerial communication. This is the "theory" behind the applications provided and discussed. Again, we will avoid technical jargon.

Managerial and leadership communication encompass a range of communication practices found in a variety of correspondence and reports—oral and written. These include informational messages, persuasive messages, and instructional messages. I focused on the neuroscience of certain kinds of instructional messages in *How the Brain Processes Multimodal Technical Instructions* (2015) and the neuroscience of certain kinds of persuasive messages in *The Neuroscience of Multimodal Persuasive Messages* (2017). Persuasion involves different neural dynamics than cognition related to instruction does.[12, 13, 14] So, it is important to distinguish the dynamics relative to the message and situation.

However, persuasion is involved in some respect even in informational and instructional messages. For example, while the purpose of this book is instructional, my educational background may influence (or persuade) a reader to believe my statements in this book more than if I had very little education. Even in an informational message, I may need to convince the audience implicitly that a statement is accurate, unless the audience already knew of the statement's accuracy. An executive who is communicating the implementation of a new business strategy can state that the transition will go smoothly, but what has he or she done to earn the audience's trust? In order for the message to be effective (believed), the audience must trust the messenger. Just as an executive looks for evidence of results by reviewing financial data, the affected audience looks for evidence of trustworthiness before it is persuaded that the statement is true.

Your belief system and values strongly influence how you may be persuaded to do something. One who does not value money, for example, will not be persuaded by an economic reward such as a bonus or raise to do something. The general focus of persuasion is to change one's attitude or beliefs about a given topic or issue or to elicit a stronger conviction in belief or attitude about that topic or issue. Managerial and leadership communication often involves communicating change to employees: changing a policy, procedure, or the way people perceive a situation toward helping improve efficiency and operations. Understanding the audience's background with variables that could influence a decision, such as culture, motivations, and values, will enable the communicator to affect neural activity to moving the audience a certain way.

For example, one concept of neuroscience we will consider in this book is that of the "mirror neurons." *Mirror neurons* are involved in helping us understand how to mirror an activity we are watching someone else do or an attribute that we value in another person. This mirroring can include sharing a perception (shared emotion) as well as with copying or imitating action. As Pillay notes, "…our brains can mirror not only actions, but intentions as well."[15] Members of the team you lead will perceive a situation in ways similar to how they think a manager perceives it, as their brain mirrors the supervisor's perception of the situation.

Persuasion

It is important to understand some concepts of persuasion, because they provide much of the basic communication-related components linking persuasion and neuroscience. Aristotle introduced the primary foundation of persuasion, and Perelman and Olbrechts-Tyteca modified that foundation to account for less scientific aspects of reasoning.[16]

A basic premise of persuasion is that the audience is willing to change their perception of a given issue. If people hold to a given position with considerable conviction, it is almost impossible to change their minds. For example, I received a mailing from an auto dealership announcing a promotion to buy a car from them a short time after I had purchased a new car. I was not in the market to buy another new car; almost no sales pitch or car commercial would have been able to motivate me to buy a new car. If the pitch or commercial is to have any real effect, one needs to be willing to consider such a purchase. A challenge for managers and leaders may be that employees do not think a change is needed, until they are made aware of the problem.

One can, also, use a variety of approaches to persuade an audience: these include logos (reason or logic), ethos (speaker's or writer's credibility), and pathos (appeal to emotion). For the most part, scholarship finds that a combination of approaches works best. For example, a physician who is trained in treatments of cancers states that many studies find a link between smoking cigarettes and lung cancer; the audience understands the physician to be trained in what causes cancers and trusts that the physician is speaking the truth (ethos: we trust the physician because of her training and expertise; we believe her to be a credible source). Further, because the physician indicates that many studies that are reported in reputable journals find that link, it is reasonable to make the conclusion about cause (smoking cigarettes) and effect (lung cancer)—(logos: if multiple studies that experts in the physician's profession believe used good research approaches reached the same conclusions, the conclusions about the link must be accurate). That message combines ethos and logos.

One's perception of a speaker or writer is influenced by culture and experience, both of which affect neurons in certain ways. Speakers who share cultural values or experiences with an audience may be able to convey a message more persuasively than a speaker who does not share an experience or value. Similarly, an audience that does not share an attitude about something with a speaker will not respond to a message that emphasizes that attitude.

A wealthy person who spent a night on a street and did not eat for 2 days may, for example, claim to understand the experience of poverty and homelessness. One person may believe that, never having experienced a night on the street or hunger from not eating for 2 days. Someone who has lived in poverty and been homeless for some time may not believe that statement, though. The wealthy person knew the experience was only for a short time and would be able to return home and eat whenever she wanted to.

Managerial Communication and Science

Neurons help to process messages and experiences generally toward helping us understand them. However, biological attributes of cognition are almost never considered in the discussion of business communication. An understanding of the processes the brain experiences can help to design more effective messages.

An executive may be most concerned with the product or outcome of a project, especially if he is trying to encourage some autonomy and independent thinking among his employees. However, the executive may want to know how the person or team "got it done" effectively afterwards; so, they understand an approach that worked well. While the product was the material outcome of the work or process of solving the problem, the process itself becomes valuable to understand for future reference because it was successful.

In this book, I use neurobiological terminology to explain why certain messages work well. The literature review related to these terms provided here avoids thick descriptions of these studies. For example, while I describe relevant concepts such as "mirror neurons" (to which I alluded earlier in this chapter), I do not refer to specialized terms given to neuron types or those of a particular region of the brain such as "F5 neurons." You do not need to be a biologist to understand how to use an understanding of neuroscience to convey messages effectively.

Four specific concepts connected to neurobiology and linked to business communication are: 1) multimodality of neurons, 2) "reward neurons," 3) "mirror neurons," and 4) neural plasticity. Further, another important term is the Colavita visual dominance effect, a concept prominently studied in neuroscience scholarship. Neurophysiologists also recognize the important role of previous experience and knowledge in cognition and perception as well as how information is presented relative to modes involved and timing of presentation, as Moreno & Mayer found.[17] These ideas are associated with the concepts of plasticity and multimodality of neurons.

Multimodality of Neurons

Neurobiologists identify two kinds of neurons relative to modal attributes: unimodal and multimodal. **Unimodal neurons** carry information relative to a single modality. For example, a unimodal auditory neuron can process only one kind of sensory information—sound. When someone reads an e-mail message or a letter, only visual information is processed. **Multimodal neurons** can carry information related to more than one mode; for example, visual and auditory. Those attending a meeting, for example, experience the speaker's voice as well as visual, nonverbal dynamics that may affect the impact of the message.

Understanding the existence of such neurons helps to understand how to use certain communication tools in different settings; an oral presentation, for example, involves visual, auditory, and spatial sensory stimuli. People in an audience see the presenter's facial expressions, body movement, and visual aids; they also hear the presenter speaking, including any changes in tone, pace, and volume; and they observe how the presenter uses the space in the room. Neurons are processing all of this information; some neurons are able to process all three stimuli while others focus on certain stimuli.

Studies related to multimodal neurons also suggest that certain kinds of information can be processed at different rates by such neurons, suggesting an optimal combination integrating various modes.[18, 19] For example, neurobiologists have studied the ***Colavita visual dominance effect*** considerably. Specifically, this phenomenon finds that information presented visually (through graphics or demonstration, for example) is processed more quickly than other kinds of delivery (text, spoken word, for example). Many scholars in cognitive psychology recognize value in presenting information both visually and aurally (see, for example, Moreno and Meyer 1999 and Mayer 2001). The combination involves multiple modes of representation that reinforce each other. Multimodal neurons can facilitate processing of information presented in the combination.

Visual-Dominance Effect

While neurons can process information from a variety of sensory modalities—vision, auditory, haptic (touch), smell—visual information is acquired the fastest; that is, the brain senses visually provided information faster than it perceives any other kind of source. Most people tend to prefer visual representations over other modalities; given a choice between watching an event on television or listening to it on the radio, most people would choose watching it on television. People can process the information about what is happening much more easily when they watch the event than when hearing someone describe it. It takes much too long to describe the entire action verbally.

Neuroscience scholarship finds that vision is the dominant sense in humans.[20, 21, 22] Colavita found in a series of four experiments that subjects responded to visual stimuli before they responded to any other sensory stimulus. Further, he notes that scholarship generally recognizes that people "do not respond as effectively to two simultaneously presented stimuli as to the same two stimuli presented in succession."[23] However, Spence, Parise, and Chen suggest that this effect is attributable to the fact that the visual information is received, generally, before any other information—auditory or touch, for example.[24] Since vision often is the first sense that receives information it, naturally, is engaged immediately; however, auditory information is processed faster than visual information.

Neuroscience recognizes the value of visual representations in facilitating cognition. This book deals with visual representations in business communication through the written word. Writing is involved in generating visual aids for oral presentations as well as in print exchanges of communication such as e-mail, letters, and reports. The visual is also involved, of course, in oral presentations and in-person meetings outside of writing; a person's presence engages visual information. A speaker's dress and physical demeanor can influence perception. Some messages are better presented in-person than in writing. We will consider some such instances later in the book.

Reward Neurons

Certain neurons are stimulated when one perceives a reward or a reason to do something. These neurons enhance the audience's attention by conveying motivation to act a certain way. This is why advertisers often integrate sex into commercials; it activates reward neurons. People pay closer attention when those neurons are activated. Reward neurons are involved in persuasive messages when a speaker acknowledges some benefit the audience may experience.

Rewards can take many forms. For example, I may receive some financial benefit—a bonus; or I may feel that I am even more a part of a certain social group; or I may feel good about helping someone else. These motivate me to act a certain way, because I perceive I will be rewarded somehow. Further, the perception of these as rewards are affected by my culture and upbringing.

Mirror Neurons

As I mentioned before, **mirror neurons** facilitate much of the cognition associated with watching someone do something and doing it yourself. When you went through training at your workplace or an internship, you watched others doing certain tasks. Your mirror neurons were active as you observed this activity. Eventually, you began to mirror those actions or behaviors. However, mirror neurons also are involved in persuasion. An audience wants to mirror some aspect of the speaker, or the speaker may want to reflect some quality of the audience to assimilate with it more. As such, mirror neurons behave differently in persuasive exchanges than they do in instructional exchanges. As I noted before in the brief description of mirror neurons, they help facilitate a shared experience between speaker and audience.[25]

Neural Plasticity

"**Neural plasticity** pertains to the ability of neurons to change their composition and behaviors relative to the information they process and experiences."[26] Through our various experiences, our neurons change to help us understand how to respond to various situations we encounter. These experiences not only change us cognitively; they change us biologically. Our neurons grow and change with these experiences, facilitating transmission of information we have learned.

Two parts of the brain closely connected to plasticity are the amygdala and the hippocampus. I describe more about these later.

Humanities scholars such as Gee, Pinker, and Mayer recognize that experience plays a role in learning about information and values.[27, 28, 29] Neurobiologists understand this link as well. Berlucchi and Buchtel define neural plasticity as:

> ...changes in neural organization which may account for various forms of behavioral modifiability, either short-lasting or enduring,

including maturation, adaptation to a mutable environment, specific and unspecific kinds of learning, and compensatory adjustments in response to functional losses from aging or brain damage (p. 307).[30]

The brain can process information more quickly as it learns more about information. With each experience individuals have with a given problem or setting, they adapt their behavior such that they eventually act on that problem or situation without thinking about it.

Because plasticity is affected by social interaction over time, culture also impacts persuasive communication. As mentioned earlier, a particular message may have a better persuasive effect in one culture but not another merely because of social expectations and perceptions of rewards or attributes of the product itself. There is a special connection between culture and perception because of how our brain responds to cultural influences. However, some of our responses are simply natural.

Hippocampus

The *hippocampus* in our brains stores information about our experiences. Was the experience positive or negative? How did we react? Did we react appropriately? Did something good happen from the way we reacted? If not, how can we change our reaction so when we experience it again we know to respond that way? Our responses are culturally determined through previous social experiences. Each time I do something somewhat new at work and receive positive feedback from my supervisors or peers (whose feedback I value), I understand that my response to the new situation was appropriate. Over time, then, I respond that same way in similar situations.

Amygdala

We have a very basic desire for self-preservation. This desire impacts responses to people or events that we do not understand or that we did not like. Certain people and events invoke fear in us, dissuading us from doing them in the future. This fear helps to preserve us by discouraging us from doing something that may harm us.

The *amygdala* is part of the brain that monitors and facilitates responses related to these basic desires. The amygdala helps us to stay alive—self-preservation. When we encounter something new that may be dangerous to us, the amygdala sends signals to the brain. Consider how many children younger than 4 years old, for example, become upset when they sit on Santa's lap at a store. They cling to the parent, not wanting to leave the safety of their parent's touch while being placed on a stranger's lap. The child responds with fear, grabbing what it knows will protect it. Plasticity is part of this dynamic. As we experience events that affected us negatively, we remember the situation and our response; and we try to avoid them in the future. Just as plasticity helps to reinforce positive experiences, it reinforces negative ones as well. Our neurons associate that event or person with fear.

Medial Prefrontal Cortex

The *prefrontal cortex* is involved in complex cognitive functions such as decision making. Several of the concepts listed here are integrated into dynamics that occur within the prefrontal cortex (PFC). One that is important but not considered in many communication texts is trust. Stimuli connected to trust between two people have been found to be processed in the medial prefrontal cortex. Zach reported on studies that identify links between trust, neuroscience, and action.[31] A few of the recommendations he makes to link management and trust are included in the considerations I formulate in this book. Indeed, as indicated earlier in this chapter, how an audience perceives the communicator affects their perception of the message itself. In rhetoric scholarship, this is called "ethos," or the speaker's credibility. In other words, an audience will consider how trustworthy the speaker conveying the message is. The more trustworthy the audience perceives the communicator, the more the message itself will be valued.

A Useful Formula for Integrating Neuroscience into Messages

So, how can we use this information to develop effective messages? Much of it revolves around getting to know your audience better than you have been encouraged to do before. Talk more with each employee to under-stand his concerns and values, for example. Apply the various concepts of neuroscience more explicitly to your consideration of the audience as you plan a message. You understand the situation and how you want your audience to respond to it. Consider your audience's needs—not just in terms of information (which has been the focus of audience analysis) but in terms of motivations, mirroring, fears, and delivery of the message.

There is a fifth element—"me." "Me" would be the speaker or writer of the message; it is embedded in the other four elements implicitly. That is, the situation is based on your perception of it as are the audience's needs and the message itself. The desired response or outcome is relative to your own perception of a desirable response or outcome. You can try to consider the situation and others as objectively as possible, but all are affected by your perception. This perception is explicitly integrated in the "audience's needs," for example. Another attribute of "me" is your own concerns about a situation and fears associated with it and the audience's response to your message. These affect what information you decide to include—and what not to include.

Any information associated with the situation and your own concerns that is irrelevant to or would negatively impact the desired response of the audience should be omitted. A problem many undergraduate business students have is that, when given a scenario to which they must respond with a message, they try to integrate as many of the details as possible, even when some of those details will negatively affect the message. Busi-ness students and managers at all levels need to learn what information is irrelevant as well as what information may hurt the impact of the mes-sage. I address some of these issues later in this book.

From the consideration of these attributes; the message is not just a set of words written or spoken, either. The message is the entirety of the presentation—including the delivery.

The message formula:

Situation--→ Desired Action or Response--→ Audience's Needs--→ Message

Table 1.1 Questions for assessing audience needs

Rewards:	Mirroring:
What will motivate this person to respond a certain way (What reward can I offer?)? How can I phrase the message so that reward is explicitly stated?	What does the audience think of me (including my trustworthiness)? What of my attributes or qualities does the audience value or admire? How can I appeal to that perception? What attributes or qualities of my audience do I value or admire? How can I integrate those into my message? What terms can I use that my audience values and will get their attention?
Fears:	Mode of Delivery:
What about this situation may invoke fear in my audience? Do I want to raise fear to provide some kind of motivation toward action? How can I defuse or minimize that fear for my audience? To what from their experiences might my audience compare this situation, and how can I help them overcome that fear or the fear they experienced before?	How can I best deliver this message to get the desired response from my audience? Writing—letter or e-mail? [print-linguistic text only] Phone call? [aural only] In person? [multimodal]

Table 1.1 summarizes questions to ask in regard to audience needs.

Specific responses to these questions will depend considerably on the specific context and audience. Indeed, a context may not need to involve all of these questions; many will involve asking only a few.

Application

At the beginning of the chapter, we considered a case about an exchange between you as a manager and an employee. Let's consider some additional factors that would impact the desirable outcome. The employee responded favorably to your message, largely because you integrated elements associated with rewards, mirroring, fears, and mode of delivery.

The exchange occurred via e-mail largely because the employee usually works a different schedule than yours and made the query via e-mail. Much communication between you and the employee occurred via e-mail in that setting. You could not expect the employee to be able to meet with you, so you responded via e-mail, though an in-person meeting would have worked just as well or better.

In the response, you described the link between the objective of efficiency and grading performance. The "penalty" for violating the standard seemed to be what prompted the employee's message; so, you addressed it. You acknowledged that the work could be performed very well using the stated approach, which is shown to be more efficient. Then, you linked the "rule" about efficiency to leadership. You stated:

> *From a leadership perspective, I would encourage you not to set out to break established and articulated rules. The rules may be in place for very good reasons. I know that some leadership books encourage "breaking the rules" to be a great leader. However, they tend to differentiate between when to break rules and when not to. They also encourage breaking rules to change a routine that is shown not to be effective. An example of "breaking the rules" appropriately with this job would be to ignore the strategies conveyed in the examples used in training while staying within, or very close to, the stated time limit. Again, efficiency was an important part of performance. Don't break the rules by ignoring a desired outcome.*

This passage integrates the reward concept as well as the fear concept. The reward is learning when to break rules and when not to; the fear element is in breaking them the wrong way or at the wrong time. It also integrates some element of mirroring. You acknowledge your own familiarity with leadership development books. You have leadership training as does the employee; you and the employee are somewhat equal in that sense. You even suggest an appropriate way to have "broken the rules" without violating the standard of efficiency. Just after this passage, you acknowledged your own leadership training experience. This furthers the mirroring. As one aspiring to become a leader, the employee values your leadership development experience.

The employee acknowledged in his message that, had he known his actions would negatively affect his performance review he would have made an effort to stay with the stated approach. Later in your message you ask a few questions pertaining to why the employee decided to break the rules if he could have made the effort to stay within the parameters in the first place. Finally, linking the questions to leadership, you state:

> *From a leadership perspective, meet the challenge (efficiency within the task, in this case) head on, and don't be afraid to make an error. The value of errors is in how much we learn from them. A good leader should not be afraid to make errors. Obviously, we hope the errors don't ruin us or the organization we lead; and we strive to learn from those lessons what to do as well as what not to do.*

Again, this engages the mirroring concept of what leadership training includes and encourages. The employee comes away from your message feeling as though he is on equal terms with you while you have also been able to "mentor" the aspiring leader regarding leadership lessons. This is the desired response, brought about by applying the concepts associated with the formula and guiding questions about audience.

The following chapters describe how the formula and concepts apply to various principles of business communication, particularly written communication, and how the reader can apply them to a variety of situations. Many of these principles echo principles of lean communication—optimizing conciseness, clarity, and effect of the message. In the following chapter, I link the formula and concepts to basic principles of business writing. In subsequent chapters, we will consider specific applications of this formula in specific contexts, especially regarding the audience consideration questions, and extend the application to other similar situations you may face.

CHAPTER 2

Basic Principles of Managerial Writing: Links to Neuroscience

As indicated in the first chapter, this book includes consideration of several forms of managerial communication. This chapter and the following two will focus on basic elements of business communication including writing style and correspondence (memos, letters, and e-mails), which includes persuasive and informational messages and proposals. These tend to be the most frequently occurring forms of written communication at leadership and managerial levels. These chapters also cover some basics of format. Format contributes a certain visual appeal to a message. Not only does it make it look more professional, like wearing a business suit to an interview instead of wearing pajamas, but it also makes information more easily accessible to the reader.

The chapters also include tips pertaining to concise phrasing. This is an important part of managerial writing as economy of words is valued by readers. Business students learn various principles of economics: transaction, value, supply, demand, and pricing, for example. Communication involves a transaction between the speaker or writer and audience. In business settings, while word supply is high, the audience demands to have read few words. The audience values phrasing that uses few words to make a meaningful impact. So, constantly try to reduce the number of words you use to phrase a given message without losing meaning or impact.

In this book, we will see that there is a balance between concise phrasing and appealing to neural attributes of the audience. While a statement may be able to be phrased using fewer words, that phrasing may have a weaker neural impact than if one integrates longer phrasing that may appeal more effectively to neural dynamics. I illustrate this with a few examples in this chapter, and you will see other examples in subsequent chapters. I also show some links between these concepts and the neuroscience concepts we considered in the previous chapter.

Perspectives

A running theme of managerial communication is that, generally, the message should appeal somehow to the reader or audience. This usually involves understanding the audience's perspective and phrasing from that perspective rather than your own perspective. Writer perspective considers only the writer's concerns; it does not include consideration of the reader's needs or position. Reader perspective considers information that the reader needs and also the readers' potential response to certain phrasing.

These considerations are explicitly included in the formula presented in the first chapter of this book. Instead of linking these considerations to information needs and emotional response, the audience considerations provided within the formula link more closely and explicitly with neural phenomena affecting both information needs and emotional response relative to mirroring and rewards.

Situation: Someone has won a contest; the award he earned is a $200 payment in the form of a check. Upon learning of his winning the award, he asks, "When will I get the check?"

An example of writer perspective is: "I sent that check out yesterday."

The writer considers that she is "done" with the act of sending the person the check when she places it in the mail. She is not worried about the reader's position in the equation. The message here is, "I took care of my responsibility yesterday." The reader understands that a check is in the mail, but he has no idea when to expect to receive it.

Reader perspective would include consideration of the fact that the reader wants to know when he will receive the check—when his reward will arrive, not when it was placed in the mail.

The reader perspective message would be, "You should receive the check within the next 2 days." The reader understands when he can expect to receive the check; the message answers his question directly.

A message can combine writer perspective and reader perspective: "I sent that check out yesterday; so, you should receive it within 2 days." Another example of this combination is the statement, "I understand how frustrating your experience was." This, generally, would appear early in an adjustment message (response to a claim message) as an effort to mirror the reader's perspective and show sympathy and empathy.

Expressing empathy disarms the reader a bit by placing the writer on a similar level while not challenging the reader's feelings about his experience. The reader may feel respected and his feelings valued. If a writer (or speaker) of such a message added an example of an experience she faced to show empathy, that would appeal directly and explicitly to the audience's mirror neurons, and the audience's reward neurons may become more active considering that he may be compensated quickly and fairly because of a shared experience and understanding of how it felt.

Another, more involved, example of the difference between writer perspective and reader perspective is the situation wherein one rejects another's proposal. One can merely state "I'm not interested." Or "No." The second is writer perspective at its most concise form. How do you react to such a statement if you are on the receiving end of it?

Compare those statements to one that integrates a few principles of reader perspective and audience considerations included in the formula. Better, yet, compare your reaction from that writer perspective statement to your reaction to this:

> Your proposal is reasonable; however, the cost exceeds our budget requirements for the project. If you can meet our budget requirements while addressing the problem, you can have the job. Thank you for your bid.

The statement is much longer than the ultraconcise, "No." However, it offers much more appeal to the audience in terms of information needs and emotional response:

1. It recognizes the audience's prior experiences in developing such proposals and pricing the work. It also, offers a positive statement reinforcing that the price is reasonable.
2. It offers a motivation to meet the stated requirements, perhaps activating reward neurons—"If you can meet…"
3. It ends thanking the reader for the work they put into the bid, suggesting valuing of that work.

4. At the same time, its conciseness comes from not repeating all that is wrong or right with the proposal and not repeating or laboring the company's needs. The reader already knows about those; not repeating them eliminates up to 20 words from the statement.

In short: it concisely helps the reader understand why the proposal is declined while facilitating a more positive emotional response than one would have from either of the writer perspective statements.

While the message usually should be phrased from the reader's perspective, there are times when writer perspective is more appropriate. These include claim letters, query messages, and messages in which some urgency is needed. Compare "I need to know your response by March 20," versus "When you have a minute, I would like to know what you think." Urgency is conveyed with writer perspective.

The principle of reader perspective appears throughout this book, and the formula engages it considerably. However, the formula also allows for some elements of writer perspective.

Positive Language and Negative Language

The way a message is phrased can affect not only how it is perceived but how the entire situation is perceived. In the example above, the message ends hopefully even though it is a rejection. This gives it a positive effect. Also, it includes acknowledgment that the proposal is reasonable. This also is a positive attribute of the message. More space is spent on the positive attributes (reasonable proposal, hope that the decision may be changed) of the message or situation than on the negative (cost is too high, rejection). So, it can be perceived more positively than if it emphasized the negative aspects.

Compare the preceding message with: "Your bid is too high; so, we're rejecting your proposal." Which would you rather read or hear? Both messages convey rejection; but the audience's response to each is likely to differ. The second message, while much more concise, offers no hope for a change of mind or the possibility for reconsideration of another bid from that company.

Case 2.1 Positive Language and Negative Language

Background

Managers are routinely asked for letters of reference or recommendations to help employees find new jobs or to help them get into a professional development program or graduate studies program. These are relatively easy to write when the employee is a good one. However, saying "no" to an employee who has not left a good impression on you poses a challenge. How you respond could leave the employee with a bad attitude toward you and, possibly, the company and its work.

Situation

A former employee whom you supervised has written you an e-mail message asking you to write a letter of recommendation for him. He states in his message that the recommendation letter is needed in order for him to gain acceptance into a particular academic program which would help advance his career.

However, you recall that this person was frequently late to work, submitted paperwork late, misinterpreted several of your instructions, and seemed to be more concerned about his social life than about the job he was to perform.

Tasks

1. Consider the strengths and weaknesses of these responses. Which is best? Worst?

   Response A

   Dear Steve:

   Thanks for thinking of me as you put together application materials for the program. Congratulations on your effort to improve yourself professionally. I am not able to write the letter you request, though.

You were frequently late to work, submitted paperwork late, misinterpreted instructions and were more concerned about your social life than work. Consequently, I cannot, in good conscience, recommend you for that program.

Good luck with your application.

Response B

Dear Steve:

Thanks for thinking of me as you put together application materials for the program. Congratulations on your effort to improve yourself professionally. I am not able to write the letter you request, though. I had several concerns about your performance.

Good luck with your application.

Response C

Dear Steve:

Thanks for thinking of me as you put together application materials for the program. I am not able to write the letter you request, though.

I did not think you were a good employee. If I write that letter, and your professors find that you are not a good student, my reputation will be hurt. I am not willing to risk that.

Good luck with your application.

Response D

Dear Steve:

Thanks for thinking of me as you put together application materials for the program. Congratulations on your effort to improve yourself professionally. I am not able to write the letter you request, though. It has been awhile since you worked for us.

I encourage you to find someone who is more knowledgeable about your current work history and performance to write that letter.

Good luck with your application.

2. Develop a "best" response; you might use elements from any of the preceding examples or compose your own original message (Make up the name and address information.).

Let's practice with using positive language and negative language. How would you respond to the situation in the following case?

Writing Proficiency

Google the term "college graduates can't write" and you can review articles identifying and describing weaknesses in the writing skills of college graduates and how these weaknesses affect hiring and promotions. Some of these articles are written by employers or report findings from surveys of employers. Google the term "skills employers seek" and you will find that in many surveys of employers, communications skills are among the top three skills hiring managers emphasize.[1, 2, 3] In fact, Simonds[4] reports that employees with strong writing skills tend to earn more promotions than those with weak writing skills.

In an interesting scholarly article, Joseph Williams[5] notes that writing errors and their impact are relative to the reader's perception of them. That is, how does a reader respond to an error in the writing, if at all? Often in business, if customers or users of a product or service do not notice a minor flaw or defect or do not experience a problem with it, that flaw or defect is not a real problem. However, when it is identified as a defect, the company's reputation has been damaged to some degree, and the company has to do something to regain the consumers' confidence.

Williams stated that most readers who are not grading your writing may not notice many small errors and not be bothered by most that they see. In some of these cases, the reader may have the same understanding of grammar usage that the writer has, even though that understanding is incorrect. For example, if the writer and reader both consider "it's" to be the possessive form of "it," then the reader will not consider the use to be an error at all (e.g., "The company's profits are down, because it's sales are too low."). Please note, though: "it's" is the contraction for "it is" ("Do not sit in that chair; it's broken."). "Its" is the possessive form of "it" ("The chair is broken; one of its legs is cracked."). If the writer makes an error AND the reader does not consider it to be an error, it's not a problem.

Lessons About Proficient Writing

The main lesson from these three points (graduates can't write, employers seek those with writing skills, and reader perception or nonperception of errors) is that, while many readers of your writing may not catch all of your writing errors, many employers value good writing skills and are able to catch obvious grammar, spelling, and punctuation errors. The neuroscientific connection to valuing good writing skills pertains to mirror neurons. The executive reader or audience values professionalism and attention to detail, which may be reflected in writing proficiency; such a person may perceive errors in writing to reflect sloppiness or lack of attention to detail. A document or message that demonstrates good proficiency with writing skills mirrors the reader's values. Writing that may include errors that a reader cannot identify mirrors the reader's skills or understanding of writing proficiency.

Invest in learning rules of grammar and addressing topics that you still struggle with. Avoid any errors that you can avoid (proofread carefully; you may catch some of your own errors). Keep in mind that some errors may slip through, though they may or may not be identifiable to your reader. The more errors your reader can identify, the more you will be perceived as unprofessional or sloppy and your professional reputation may be hurt. Others may perceive that you do not mirror their professional values.

Conciseness and Clarity

Two attributes valued highly in business communication are conciseness and clarity. The concept of economics in business settings characterizes efficient use of supplies and processes to produce goods. Manufacturers use supplies efficiently, getting the most out of the supplies and processes to produce goods at a low cost so that they can be sold at a low cost. Efficiency means that good quality products are produced at low cost.

If a company "cuts corners," or eliminates a necessary supply item or procedure, it may produce a product at low cost; however, the product is of poor quality. This is not a good outcome in economic terms. If a company does not use necessary supplies and processes efficiently, a good quality product may be produced but at high cost. This, also, is not good in economic terms.

The term "conciseness" in communication means to use words economically to make meaning. A former professor of mine once encouraged students to be concise with the mantra: "Every word works." It means that every word you use should do something to make meaning. Do not use more words than you need to use to make meaning. However, use enough words so that meaning is not lost. As with efficiencies encouraged in other lean processes, conciseness, clarity, and impact are implicitly linked to lean communication.

Using too many words is inefficient; the audience has to do more work than they should have to, and so does the author. A statement that uses too many words is considered to be "wordy." It could be phrased more concisely.

Using too few words also is inefficient because the audience does not understand the message's meaning well. A statement that uses too few words may be considered "blunt." It may come across as rude or just lacking sufficient information to make the meaning clear.

Conciseness actually is not unique to managerial or business writing; it is important in academic writing as well. However, many students perceive that academic writing includes a lot of "fluff" or unnecessary information or wording. If you met a word requirement for an essay by including "fluff," you did not do the assignment well. You likely had many sentences that were "wordy." Or you perceived that information detailing your research and analysis was "fluff" when it was not. Consider that the purpose of the essay was to demonstrate knowledge, analytical skills, and organizational skills, as well as proficient language skills. Such a piece of writing will need to be longer than when addressing the purpose of correcting a problem at work.

So, conciseness is not a feature distinguishing academic writing from business writing; however, the length of a piece of writing will likely differ between business writing and academic writing because of the audience and purpose involved. Because of its purpose, a piece of academic writing tends to be longer than a piece of business writing.

"Concise" and "blunt" both pertain to the length of a message, typically characterizing it as short and to the point. However, "blunt" implies insensitivity, lack of clarity (there is not enough information to help the audience understand the message clearly), or a negative connotation associated with the brevity of the message. It is not the same thing as "concise."

"Concise" implies that the message avoids using unnecessary words and maintains a good rhetorical effect without losing its meaning. There is an economy of words.

"Tact" has nothing to do with the length of a message; though, the message should be phrased concisely. "Tact" implies that the message sounds nice by emphasizing positive attributes of the message, even though the overall message is negative. Here are some examples to illustrate these points.

Example 1:
Wordy: The accountants calculated the Net Profit Margin ratio, Return on Assets ratio, and Return on Equity ratio so that management could assess the company's profitability for the past year. (29 words)

> *Is there a way to categorize some items? (How about those ratios?)*
> *Is there a way to eliminate unnecessary words? (Who usually assesses efficiency or performance?)*

Concise: The accountants provided several ratios to facilitate assessment of the company's profitability last year. (14 words)

> *While there are more ratios that can be used to assess performance generally; those listed focus more on profitability.*
> *Also upper management or executives usually assess profitability and would likely know the ratios the company uses.*

Blunt: The accountants prepared the ratios necessary to assess performance. (9 words)

Again, more ratios can be used to assess performance; so, need to clarify. What unit's profitability is being assessed (entire company? particular unit within company?) What period is being assessed?
Unless those items are indicated prior to this statement, that information is lacking.

Example 2:

Wordy and vague: The marketing department should review historical sales data and perform statistical analyses on that data to find out whether periodic sales trends of our products can be forecasted. (28 words)

What specific kind of statistical analysis is suggested in this passage?

Concise: The marketing department should use regression analysis to ascertain whether we can forecast periodic sales of our products.

(18 words)

"Regression analysis" characterizes the statistical analysis suggested in the previous passage. Also, note some rephrasing to cut words after "to."

Blunt: The marketing department needs to determine whether sales can be forecasted based on trends. (14 words)

This passage does not specify a particular statistical or quantitative kind of trend analysis, and a reader might not think to use regression analysis.

Case 2.2 Using Conciseness and Tact

Situation

Drawing on the recommendation letter scenario included earlier in the chapter, let's assume that you approach a professor by e-mail with a request for a letter of recommendation for a job application, and the professor responds via e-mail:

Question: Would you write a letter of recommendation for me?

Response A: No.

Response B: You're a good student; but, as a policy, I do not write letters of recommendation for students. Good luck with your application.

Response C: I have not gotten to know your strengths well enough to be able to provide a letter of recommendation.

Tasks

1. Which response would you prefer to receive? Why?
2. Which response would you characterize as concise as opposed to blunt?
3. Which response is most tactful?

Discussion

All three responses carry the same message; you're not getting a letter of recommendation from the writer. However, the message is conveyed three different ways. Further, you react to each message differently.

Given these characterizations:

Response A is blunt but clear in responding to your request. However, you do not understand why the professor will not write a letter of recommendation for you; is it something you should be concerned about in your performance? Is it a general policy of the professor? If you value that information mirror neurons are not activated. Further, you do not know whether to fear that your performance is the cause.

Response B is tactful and applies reader perspective well. Reward neurons may be activated as may mirror neurons. You feel a bit better about the situation; though, you are not getting the letter your requested.

Response C is concise and uses writer perspective. The professor cannot write the letter, because she does not know what she could write about your strengths. Your amygdala is satisfied that your performance is not the issue.

Case 2.3 Replies that Satisfy

Background

Admissions departments at academic institutions tend to want a recommender to respond to questions concerning a number of abilities of an applicant. These include, but are not limited to, leadership, ability to work in teams, communication skills, critical thinking skills, independent thinking skills, analytical skills, and motivations for learning and for succeeding. A requester may or may not be aware of these characteristics in the applicant.

Situation

Consider Response C in Case 2.2: "I have not gotten to know your strengths well enough to be able to provide a letter of recommendation." It omits acknowledgment about what information admissions people want. Is this message clear and concise? Consider neuroscientific attributes associated with the message: is there anything that activates reward neurons? Mirror neurons? Allays fear?

Tasks

1. If you were the one requesting the letter, would you be satisfied with Response C (beyond the disappointment of not getting the recommendation)?
2. How would you phrase it to be clearer and elicit neuroscientific response, if at all?

Interacting with Professionals

Much of the information in this book makes explicit reference to written communication or oral presentations—generally considered a bit more formal than a face-to-face interaction with one person or a very small group in a less formal encounter. However, almost all of the information can be applied to any encounter in a professional setting. For example, while you may correspond via e-mail (written communication) with someone, you may just as easily communicate via phone (oral communication) or face-to-face in your office or a hallway. The principles of perspective, conciseness, and clarity still apply.

As indicated in Chapter 1, you can even work on a message in written form knowing you may convey it in oral form. Consider an elevator pitch; business students at many institutions are encouraged to prepare an elevator pitch. They compose a script and practice it so it can be delivered orally at the right opportunity. When I was just out of graduate school and applying for jobs, I had an application letter I used regularly. Through networking, I found out about a possible job opening and contacted the main hiring manager by phone later the same day that I found out about the position. I conveyed most of my application letter over the phone, and the manager invited me in to talk about the position. The next day, I interviewed, and I was filling out employment forms that night.

One of the concepts presented in the next chapter (correspondence) is the claim message, seeking an adjustment for a defective product or service. This is a common kind of written message presented in business contexts; however, it is easily presented over the phone. So, as you read the material throughout this book, keep in mind the potential to apply it in written and oral forms.

CHAPTER 3

Correspondence and Proposals

Correspondence is the most basic form of written business communication. It takes the form of an e-mail, memo, or letter. Generally, it is addressed to one person or a small group, some of whom may be copied on the message that targets one person to whom it is principally addressed. Proposals are persuasive messages that can take the shape of correspondence (memo, e-mail proposal, or letter proposal), or as a formal separate document. This chapter includes information about these topics.

Memo

A memo is an internal message; that is, it is a message exchanged between people who work in a single organization or company. Because of this context, it generally is much shorter than a letter, perhaps only two or three paragraphs. Memos can be used to announce a new policy or procedure being implemented (a directive), to request something in particular (query message), or to request input about something toward helping make a decision.

Because it is an internal message, the writer is likely to understand the reader's needs more readily than if it were an external message. Also, various political dynamics associated with the company (office politics) may play out in an internal message. So, some portions of a message may be implicitly suggested. A directive, for example, involves vertical flow of the message from upper level to lower level; the implication is that the reader (lower level in the organization's hierarchy) is expected to act on it accordingly without challenging it.

Case 3.1 Providing a Positive Slant

Situation

A small manufacturing company has good performance from its first-and second-shift employees, but the third shift is much less productive because of relaxed enforcement of some policies. The company's management recognizes that a new policy should be implemented to assure third-shift employees are at their workstation in a timely manner.

Situation

Management might send the following memo to the five third-shift employees:

> To: Third-Shift Employees
> From: Supervisors
> Re: Clocking in Policy Enforcement
> Date: December 20, 20xx
>
> As of January 2, the clock-in policy will be vigorously enforced. All third-shift employees are to clock in by 10:45 p.m. and be at their workstation by 11 p.m. This process helps supervisors know that all stations are staffed and ready to begin in a timely manner.
>
> Violations of this policy will be noted by supervisors. The first violation will result in a warning; subsequent violations may result in wage reduction or dismissal.

The message is very concise. The new enforcement of the policy and its implementation date are indicated immediately, a short rationale is provided and penalties for violations are conveyed. The total message is all of four lines, divided into two short paragraphs. The employee understands that he or she is not to ask questions about it or suggest a different policy in response. No response, other than the stated action, is expected.

Put yourself in the reader's place. How effective is the message? The message raises fear in the employee by threatening wage reduction or dismissal; as such, the reward implied is continued employment. A reward is not explicitly stated, but punishment is explicitly stated.

The policy reflects a change in work culture, which may challenge the employees' prior experiences. If they have been allowed to get away with arriving later and not being productive, the change is a large shift in perception; they are being punished for management's behavior. If they routinely arrive late and management has been warning them but not enforcing penalties, then the message is less a surprise and more a formal action to document awareness of enforcement.

The format also contributes to the message. Memos include a "To" line, indicating the recipient(s); a "From" line, indicating the author (individual or group); the date on which it is sent out; and the subject line. The subject line is important, because it should provide the reader with a concise statement about the topic of the message. The subject line used in the previous message is effective; there is no question about the topic of the message.

Task

Do you suggest any changes to the message, its format, or how it is delivered? Why?

Revision with Neuroscience Application

The message in Case 3.1 can be phrased much better by applying elements of the neuroscience-related formula. For example, considering that there are only a handful of employees, the writer could list them by name to make the message feel a bit more personal. The message itself could be phrased to include:

We are going to begin rigorously enforcing the clock-in policy for the third shift starting January 2. Supervisors will note tardiness, and it will become part of employee performance reviews.

First and second shifts have been more productive because of enforcement of rules. Adherence to the policy may result in wage increases as part of the performance review. The first violation will result in a warning; subsequent violations may result in wage reduction or dismissal.

The message has increased to seven lines. It indicates the same treatment as the first and second shifts to engage mirror neurons; enforcement mirrors that of other shifts; so, it is considered fair and reasonable. Also, it acknowledges rewards explicitly while making the reader aware of penalties, raising some level of fear for any who may have difficulty adhering to it.

An element of office politics that may be inferred is that management has not enforced the policy for third shift because it recognizes some of the challenges and lack of appeal of third-shift work hours. Employees may understand that to be the reason why the policy was not being enforced, even if management had spoken to the employees before; but the message helps to explain why enforcement is needed. Nevertheless, the employee understands that prior experience was based on sympathy from management and may respond more favorably to the change because of that understanding. Their perception may be: "Management was being nicer to us than to other employees, because it felt badly for us. However, management's sympathy has cost the company in productivity; so, we are going to be treated as the other shifts are."

While the message is informational—announcing enforcement of an existing policy, it includes an element of persuasion. The enforcement of the policy is meant to increase productivity; so, the message attempts to persuade the reader to participate in that effort.

Letters

While memos involve internal communication, letters involve external communication; that is, letters are sent to readers who are outside of the organization or company. The reader typically is a customer or client, a supplier, or agent of some kind for the company.

Generally, letters are longer than a memo is, because they need to include more information to help the reader understand some points or background of the company or organization. Further, the writer needs to appeal somehow to the reader, and that, will take a bit more space than merely articulating our position on the matter.

Some common types of letters and what they include are summarized in Table 3.1.

Examples of each of these can be found online with a simple search using the type of message as the search term. A very detailed example of a claim message is in Chapter 5 along with the description of how the formula is applied.

The format of a letter generally includes the following parts:

(a) Heading: Address of sender and date on which it is sent (avoid numeric notation of date).

(b) Inside address: Name, title, and address of person receiving the message.

(c) Salutation: The "Dear" part. Avoid generic salutations such as "Dear Sir," "Dear Madam," "Dear Sir or Madam," and "To whom it may concern." Consider how you feel when you receive mail addressed to "Occupant."

   Punctate the salutation using a COLON. (NOTE: The comma is used in international forms of English, such as British or Canadian English; however, these also use different spelling styles for words such as color (colour) and flavor (flavour).)

(d) Letter text, with appropriate paragraphing.

(e) Closing: Complimentary close (e.g., "Sincerely," "Cordially," "Truly"). Punctuate the complimentary close using a comma. Space for signature, and typed version of sender's name.

These items and their placement are included in the example provided in Chapter 5.

The format of a letter or memo has an impact on the reader, even though it seems a mundane attribute of the message. The inclusion of formal elements (heading, inside address, salutation…) contribute to making the document look professional and clean. Again, the mirroring dynamic comes into play, because a professional-looking document mirrors an audience's professionalism. Further, particular information can be found in specific parts, and the audience knows where to access that information.

Table 3.1 Information included in common types of business letters

Kind of message or attributes	Claim	Adjustment	Query	Rejection	Sales
Purpose	Request adjustment for defective goods or services	• Address claim message • Respond to concern about defective good or service	Seek information to help with decision	Decline of request for something	Persuade reader to buy or accept something
Details to include	• Purchase date • Product or service details • How used before problem became evident; how problem was recognized • Action to address problem	• Respect for concern • Action you can take • Gesture of goodwill • Encouragement for continued patronage	• Specific questions about needed information • Why you need information (may help with phrasing response) • Date by when you need answer	• Restatement of what is being requested • Statement of rejection with concise reasoning • Encouragement	• Product or service features • How reader will benefit from using product, service, or idea • Differentiation from competing products, services, or ideas
Primary perspective	Writer perspective	Reader; though, some writer	Writer	Reader	Reader
Tone	Neutral; balance positive and negative, while trying to be more positive	Positive Recognize the person's feelings, but move on	Positive	Neutral to positive	Positive

Through composing and reading letters and applying those formal elements, neural plasticity helps to make such format an expectation. If a document is not formatted correctly, it looks odd or unprofessional. The reader knows what to expect with format, and any deviation from that expectation calls negative attention to itself, not unlike if an executive walked into a board meeting wearing sweatpants and a hoodie.

E-mail began in the form of an internal messaging system. Large companies with their own servers could connect computers through the local network associated with a particular internal; server. The server would serve as a central information storage cache, and computers connected to it could access the software and information files easily. Once these computers were linked to the central server, messages could be sent between computers. Because they were internal messages, they took on attributes of memos. That is why the e-mail header looks like a memo header.

E-mail has grown with the Internet to facilitate external messages as well. Typically, internal e-mails take on attributes of memos (for example, lacking a salutation or closing and having a concise message in a few paragraphs), while external messages take on attributes of a letter (for example, inclusion of a salutation and closing as well as longer text). As with the plasticity example previously discussed, we no longer think about the format of an e-mail; we just accept it as appropriate, whether it is an internal message or an external message.

The principles associated with the different kinds of letters or messages conveyed in the table above shape e-mail messages as well.

Difficult Situations

There are some difficult situations that require communication. For instance, you may need to respond to a request from an angry or upset person (customer, client, or coworker), and you need to do it with tact while being concise. We will consider tips for dealing with two such situations: denying of customer service and declining or rejecting a request.

Generally, managers want to portray situations positively, because employees and customers will feel better about a situation that is positive.

Positive language emphasizes the positive attributes of a message; it can identify negative attributes, but it focuses more time or space on positives. Negative language emphasizes negative attributes of the message; likewise, it may identify positive attributes, but focuses more time or space on the negatives.

Example:

Negative language: The report covers all of the important items, but there are several grammar errors and graphics are misplaced. Consequently, it is weak.

Positive language: The report has a few weaknesses, but the information is accurate and presented concisely. The graphics are also very helpful.

Neutral language: While the report covers all of the important information and has helpful graphics, there are several mechanical errors and the graphics need to be placed more appropriately.

Positive language may elicit reward neurons and allay fear while eliciting mirror neurons as well. The author of the report receives positive feedback that suggests he or she is mirroring the reader's values.

Negative language may activate the amygdala, which may be what the manager wants to do in certain cases.

Neutral language balances the two.

Customer Service

A customer has sent a claim message—via letter, e-mail, or phone—conveying a problem with a product or service you provide. Of course, you allay her concern by pointing out that you are sorry to hear or read about it and then try to do something she will find acceptable to address it. The acknowledgment of sympathy helps to elicit mirror neurons; you understand their frustration and validate how she feels. What you do about it elicits reward neurons; the customer wonders how she will benefit from how you handle it. She may be satisfied with simply receiving the replaced product or correct service. She may expect some form of compensations beyond that "fix," though. How do you appeal to both mirror neurons and reward neurons? Should you try to appeal to both?

In fact, the results are more important to the customer than your sympathy is.[1] It is not that people do not care whether you feel sorry for them; it is nice to know that others feel badly for you. However, the material outcome is more meaningful. Consider: Given a choice between receiving sympathy from someone and receiving $100 from them, most would take the $100.

So:

1. Consider focusing on a meaningful result or outcome to appease the customer.
2. Spend less time offering sympathy; it is nice, but not valued much.
3. Avoid repeating all the details from the claim message; the customer knows what happened.

This will help keep the message concise while having the desired impact from your perspective—addressing the customer's needs and making them feel better about the situation.

Declining Requests

Occasionally, one must decline a request (e.g., request for a letter of recommendation, request for a raise, request for a promotion…). Generally, use positive language by recognizing the person's strengths, but help him understand that you cannot provide what he is requesting:

1. Identify strengths and how you value him.
2. Do not spend much time on why you will not provide what he wants.
3. Offer encouragement and hope (but not false hope).

Anytime there is such a request, the person's reward neurons are very active. Give him something to respond to that desire to act. He will feel better about the outcome than if you just say "No."

Case 3.2 Saying No and Saving Goodwill

Background

You manage a group of 10 employees within your organization. Your company is small, but it has grown well over the past 5 years. You have been able to provide funding to send employees to various conferences for their professional development purposes and for the benefit of the company. Employees are able to gain new information about trends in their field and apply them in their work.

You have been in this position for 3 years. As manager, your responsibilities include budgeting for the department as well as managing personnel in the department. It is up to you to decide how to allocate funds for your department's operations. This includes salaries for employees in your department and funding professional development-related travel. You also conduct employee performance evaluations and base much of your salary decisions and allocation for professional development on those reviews. You've been able to do your job very well so far, as your company's growth and employees' development demonstrate. The assessment of your own performance and your salary depend on how much money you save of the company in addition to how well you manage your employees. Consequently, you're constantly thinking about a balance between keeping employees happy and handling various issues that affect cost efficiency.

Situation

You recently finished providing employee performance reports to your staff in preparation for next fiscal year's budget; and each got a raise of 3 percent, which is all you could afford to give them. The company is growing, but you try to set aside funds for professional development opportunities. One employee just wrote to you asking for a higher raise—7 percent more, in fact.

In her argument for the higher raise, she points out that colleagues at a recent conference indicated how much salary they make each year and what the average salary in the field is. They also indicated that in their own research, they found that the average salary for a company of your company's size is higher than what you are paying your employees. In your own performance review of the particular employee, you gave her very high assessments, indicating how valuable she is as an employee. She notes this in her argument as well and asks to be paid accordingly. She suggests that she may leave the company, making the case that she is worth more than you are paying her. This is an excellent employee, and you want to keep her happy.

Task

Develop a response to this employee's request, ***declining the request.*** Again, this is a very good employee, and you want to keep her. You really cannot give one person a higher raise without affecting other employees and their opportunities for development. Consider ways that you may be able to motivate the employee without raising her salary more than the 3 percent you have given everyone in the department. Develop any reasonable details to help you with your message.

To help with these details, complete the following Audience Consideration questionnaire based on your own responses if you were the employee.

Audience Consideration Questionnaire

Rewards:

> What will motivate this person to respond a certain way (what reward can I offer?)?
>
> How can I phrase the message so that reward is explicitly stated?

Mirroring:

> What does the audience think of me (including my trustworthiness)?
>
> What of my attributes or qualities does the audience value or admire?

How can I appeal to that perception?

What attributes or qualities of my audience do I value or admire?

How can I integrate those into my message?

What terms can I use that my audience values and will get their attention?

Fears:

What about this situation may invoke fear in my audience?

Do I want to raise fear to provide some kind of motivation toward action?

How can I defuse or minimize that fear for my audience?

To what from their experiences might my audience compare this situation, and how can I help them overcome the fear they experienced before?

Mode of Delivery:

How can I best deliver this message to get the desired response from my audience?
- Writing—letter or e-mail? [only print-linguistic text]
- Phone call? [only aural]
- In person? [multimodal]

Proposals

The purpose of a proposal is to persuade the reader to do something or accept something. Consequently, it integrates several features of persuasive rhetoric. It can be in the form of a formal report or as a form of correspondence. In a later chapter, you will see an example of a proposal in e-mail form.

Proposals vary from planning proposals (addressing a problematic situation or condition) to research proposals (requesting funding to support conducting empirical research) or sales proposals (persuading the reader to purchase a product or service). We will consider the attributes of sales proposals and planning proposals, since those are the more common types in managerial settings. Planning proposals are the more common type among executives.

Sales Proposals

A sales proposal attempts to convince the reader to purchase something. This is a regular part of a sales manager's job. Generally, the proposal should detail the product or service features and differentiate these from similar products or services offered by competitors (differentiation). This differentiation should help the reader understand how your product or service is better than that of your competitors.

The proposal should also use reader perspective; however, that is difficult to accomplish when providing information about the product or service features. To accomplish reader perspective, describe how a given feature will benefit the reader. For example, consider the statements:

The XP4 includes a faster speech recognition tool.

The XP4 includes a faster speech recognition tool; so, you can complete the transcription much faster and have more time to work on other parts of the project.

The second statement integrates reader perspective in that the benefit of a faster speech recognition tool is explicitly acknowledged. As such, it considers a potential reward of value to the audience—more productivity. Further, by suggesting value of productivity and efficiency, the statement suggests mirroring of the reader's values.

Planning Proposals

Typically, a planning proposal will call attention to a particular problem and how to address it. Management at various levels may compose these, and executives work with these on a regular basis. Such a proposal identifies the problem explicitly and describes how it is a problem (which may have the heading or subheading "Problem Identification" and "Background"). Then, a particular solution to address the problem may be detailed or several possible solutions may be detailed. These details include a description of the solution, its benefits and drawbacks, and a budget related to its implementation. Finally, a course of action is recommended and an implementation plan described.

Examples of such proposals are available online, but an outline with headings may look like this:

Introduction
        Topic and Purpose
        Problem
        Background
        Scope
Proposed Solution (if only one is provided; if more are provided each solution may represent its own section of the body, and one would be presented as the recommendation in another section detailing why that one was the best option)
        Description
        Benefits
        Drawbacks

Implementation
        Schedule
        Budget

Generally, reader perspective is best to use with any proposal. With the planning proposal this means that you should emphasize the benefits (or drawbacks, depending on their position) for the reader and why the reader should act upon the proposed solution. It also means using a persuasive approach valued by the audience. This can pertain to research approach or examples used as illustrations to develop a given point.

Pretend that you are taking classes at a large institution and you understand that the institution's full time employees and their spouse and children do not have to pay tuition to attend classes there. The tuition waiver for full time employees is 100 percent. You perceive it to be unfair that their tuition is free while you have to pay. You propose to the institution's administration to eliminate the tuition waiver entirely for employees there, using fairness as the sole basis of persuasion. You explain that it is not fair that students whose parents do not work at the university have to pay while those whose parents work there do not have to pay.

A very large percentage of institutions offer some kind of tuition benefit for full time employees, even if it is as low as 12 percent (or one course for an academic year). Several use a waiver of 50 percent, while very few have a waiver of 100 percent. However, you did not research this.

Given the relatively common use among colleges and universities of tuition fee waivers of some sort as a perk to recruit and retain quality employees, this argument to eliminate the tuition waiver entirely would not have been considered very persuasive by the university administration. University administration would, for example, want to know what comparable institutions offer and how reimbursement levels encourage or discourage professional development and personal advancement among other considerations.

Had you done some research, you could have ascertained a reasonable tuition benefit that both you and the administration would consider to be fair within the market.

Case 3.3 Proposing Persuasively

Background

Several companies provide a tuition waiver or tuition benefit for employees who are pursuing an academic degree—undergraduate and graduate level. Some, for example, reimburse employees based on academic performance while others may reimburse a certain percentage generally (not based on academic performance).

Situation

Assume you work for a company that does not provide a tuition waiver of any kind, and you have a friend who works at another company that provides a reimbursement of 50 percent. You want to propose to your company's executives to implement a tuition benefit.

- How would you approach ascertaining a fair tuition benefit (what research would you use?)
- What would the waiver or benefit be (do the research)?

- How would you integrate that information into a proposal concisely?

Task

Compose a message of not more than 200 words conveying what you think is fair, based on your research, how you came to that point, and why it should be implemented.

CHAPTER 4

Elements of Formal Reports

Formal reports and proposals will include a number of sections, each including subsections. As shown in the previous chapter, proposals involve persuasive effort to encourage an audience to implement recommendations toward addressing a problem or situation. An outline of a proposal was included in that chapter. Typical sections for a report or proposal include:

Executive Summary: Summarizes the important information for a report or proposal's contents.

Introduction: Identifies the topic or problem, purpose of the report, background, and scope.

Discussion: Develops each potential solution or discusses the single-proposed solution; reports research findings and provides analysis.

Conclusion: Identifies specific conclusions that emerged from the information presented.

Recommendation: Identifies and discusses specific recommendations and how to implement them.

Appendixes: Provide secondary or tertiary graphics or data (data that is relevant to the report but not vital to the purpose of the report; for example, statistical analyses of research data).

References: Lists all outside sources used.

Business Plans

Business plans represent a different kind of business document. Specific sections depend on the nature of the business. However, most plans will include the following:

Business Description: Identifies the legal status of the company, its background or history, and mission statement or vision statement.

Product or Services Plan: Lists and describes specific products or services the company offers.

Marketing Plan: Provides analysis of market segments, competition, competitive advantage, identifying marketing strategy, and possible tactics for target segments.

Operating Plan: Identifies suppliers, processes for operation (depends on whether a manufacturing company, retailer, service company…) facilities used, staffing needs, and other elements of the business operation.

Financial Plan: Includes pro forma (forecasted) accounting statements for periods involved. Considers various scenarios relative to the economy and business conditions (best case; worst case; most likely).

Audit Schedule: Identifies when the plan will be reviewed, with comparison of actual figures to pro forma statements, with resulting necessary adjustments.

Most reports follow these patterns of sections and organization. Such structure facilitates efficient access and presentation of information. A section or subsection may be a paragraph or more; there is no minimum or maximum length limitation to the number of paragraphs a given section or subsection may have.

Formal reports often integrate research, much as academic essays include research. The next section addresses some differences between the forms of research associated with each—business reports and academic essays.

Practical Research for Business Settings

One of the big differences between academic writing and business writing is the research required to develop points. What you learned about research for academic writing will help you understand valued research in business writing; however, the audience and context or situation affect what kinds of research are valued in business.

The academic writing you did for college classes likely involved *secondary research*. Such resources were generally considered to be authored by recognized experts on a topic or published empirical studies, either of which appeared in publications recognized as valued. *Anecdotal information* (such as something a friend said or a single experience you or a friend had) was considered less valuable, but it could be used as an example to illustrate a point. Nevertheless, you were generally expected to cite a number of outside sources.

Business people value both anecdotal as well as secondary sources; however, either needs to be **immediately relevant to the situation** and be related to that particular business or industry. So, in one situation one might be able to use only anecdotal evidence to make a point (e.g., citing two other companies in the same industry as your company that use a given social media tool a certain way within a proposal for the company to use that tool as well). In a different situation one may need to refer to secondary resources recognized as valuable to make a point (e.g., locating empirical studies showing how a certain social media tool is benefitting companies generally).

What research you use depends on the situation and the reader's perspective—what information will the reader value? By extension, then, even your approach to research integrates elements of neuroscience. By integrating research valued by the reader, you are eliciting mirror neurons relative to the audience's values.

Example

Your company is trying to reach more consumers in the 18 to 30 age demographic, and the economy is generally weak. You know your company does not use social media much for marketing, and you think using it may help with this effort. What research do you need to help support your idea?

1. If you can find two companies with which your company competes directly and that use Facebook for marketing, those may be the ONLY sources you need, and they are considered anecdotal.

   "A friend of mine works at [Competitor X] and another works at [Competitor Y], and both said they have increased sales to this demographic in the past year. The only difference in their strategy and ours is their use of Facebook this year."

   In a competitive environment, everyone is looking for ways to beat their competition, and if others in the industry are having success with a given tool, your company will want to use it, too. It wants to mirror similar companies that are having success, and that potential success elicits reward neurons.

2. If other companies in your industry are not yet using social media, you may need to look into a few empirical studies (***secondary sources***, which are published accounts of the research conducted by others) to show that Facebook is used by people in that demographic, and it is helping other companies in various industries increase sales to that demographic.

   "A study by researchers at Harvard that was reported in the magazine *Inc.* found that 80 percent of 18 to 30 year-olds use Facebook at least three times a week (citation). Another study reported in *Ad Age* found that companies using Facebook are increasing sales to that demographic (citation)."

   You will need to show evidence that it is an effective tool generally, and citing reliable sources will help with that. Generally, executives respect both *Inc.* magazine and Harvard researchers; both mirror their values—excellence in practice. Alternatively, you may be able to refer to an article published in the *Harvard Business Review*, authored by a CEO or entrepreneur who has had success with the strategy. Executives tend to respect such publications; such publications mirror their values, and executives want to mirror success of other executives.

3. If you are aware of a company in another industry that uses social media effectively, you may combine the secondary sources and that

anecdotal evidence to develop your argument to implement it at your company.

"A friend of mine who works in [different field] said her company increased sales by 20 percent to that demographic last year when they started using Facebook for marketing. Also, a study by researchers at Harvard that was reported in the magazine Inc. found that 80 percent of people in that demographic use Facebook at least three times a week (citation). Another study reported in *Ad Age* found that companies using Facebook are increasing sales to that demographic without increasing costs much (citation)."

Again, in a weak economy, you may need a few different kinds of sources to make a strong argument, depending on how big a risk your boss perceives. Again, too, this elicits reward and mirror neurons. Finally, change this scenario to a strong economy (more money available for risk taking), and you may need only anecdotal evidence.

A friend of mine who works in [different field] said her company increased sales by 20 percent to that demographic last year when they started using Facebook for marketing. So, let's give it a try. We can collect data on how well it goes, too [suggesting primary, empirical research to assess effectiveness].

The potential reward (reward neurons) outweighs the risk; so, executives may be willing to spend the money to try it.

At times you may want to gather your own first-hand information about the topic you are researching. For instance, you might conduct a survey of potential consumers in your demographic as to how much they are influenced by Facebook for making purchase decisions. This type of research gathering is referred to as ***primary research*** because you are gathering it directly.

As you look into articles in respected practitioner-oriented publications, such as *Inc., Fortune, Harvard Business Review,* and those that are published by professional organizations, you will find that many do not cite outside sources or use only interviews with executives or researchers. The content and related arguments are based entirely on the author's experience or the testimony of those executives and researchers. These represent anecdotal and general observations conveyed by people with unique experience in a leadership position.

Some of these articles report narratives of particular experiences by these leaders and executives. A narrative represents a "story" about a real experience the speaker or writer had. It includes a number of details about the experience and reflection about the experience. Readers who have had a similar kind of experience connect quickly with such narratives, because they appeal to mirror neurons. Much has been written about narrative's persuasive effects on audiences, including an article by Stephen Denning published in the *Harvard Business Review*.[1] The experience of the reader mirrors that of the respected author or executive; and the reader values that reflection.

Again, anecdote and theorization based on experience are valued by readers depending on how relevant they are to the reader's situation. Mirror neurons of managers or executives will be very active as they read of narratives, observations and tips by another executive who has been successful, especially if their success came in a similar industry.

Narrative can be an effective part of any managerial message as well. Just as it has value in practical research for describing specific applications of tactics to address a problem, it is valued as a device to develop a point. You can, for example, provide a narrative describing an experience and how that experience is problematic or is a symptom of a problem that needs to be addressed. One can use a narrative to explain why a new policy needs to be implemented. Narrative used this way helps the audience relate to the problem more clearly; they may be able to understand the experience from a similar experience they had. So, narrative may draw upon an audience's prior experiences, affecting neural activity.

Analysis

Analysis is a systematic approach to reviewing data collected through research or from observations toward identifying findings or conclusions about that data. The starting point is a problem that needs to be addressed or a decision that needs to be made about something.

Research helps us gather information that will contribute to helping us make a decision or address a problem.

Once data is collected, we need to analyze it; it is the analysis that shapes findings and conclusions. There are many forms of business analysis, including the following:

- SWOT analysis: *SWOT analysis* includes an examination of the **S**trengths, **W**eaknesses, **O**pportunities, and **T**hreats inherent to the problem under consideration. It is highly focused on competitors and market conditions and is often used when preparing a business plan.
- Cost-benefit analysis: *Cost-benefit analysis* considers the cost of implementing a new program versus the benefit of implementing it; does the benefit outweigh the cost? Cost-benefit analysis is often useful when developing the arguments in a proposal.
- Feasibility analysis: *Feasibility analysis* assesses the feasibility of a project or action relative to established criteria and conditions.
- Economic criteria analysis: *Economic analysis* examines these issues: (1) Do we have the money to build, staff, and maintain the project, and (2) Where will it come from?

Analyses facilitate ascertaining findings about the data, which directly contribute to conclusions.

Example

"80 percent of respondents indicated they would be willing to contribute to funding a parking garage."
(Analysis is based on looking at frequency of responses to a question or set of questions from a survey tool.)

Conclusion

"The data shows that students are willing to contribute to funding the construction and maintenance of a parking garage."

Conclusions and Recommendations

Many people do not understand the difference between conclusions and recommendations. Asked to identify a recommendation from a study, they will identify a conclusion.

Conclusions are based on analysis of data collected in research—be it anecdotal, published, or primary research, as shown in the previous section. Recommendations are based on conclusions AND are relative to the purpose of the report.

Using the previous example conclusion:

"The data shows that students are willing to contribute to funding the construction and maintenance of a parking garage."

If the purpose of the report is to ascertain ways to address a problem with parking, a recommendation from this conclusion would be: "Build a parking deck, and charge students $100 per semester to fund the new deck."

Recommendations can be phrased to elicit reward neurons as well. You could add the potential benefits of acting on the recommendation: "A parking deck, funded by students, will reduce congestion around campus while making the campus appear favorable to prospective students."

Executive Summary

The executive summary (sometimes referred to as an abstract) provides concise information about the most important elements of a proposal or report. At the very least, a good executive summary identifies the problem being addressed, or the topic of the report, and recommendations. Such a summary may range in length from a half page to a full page.

A longer executive summary will also include information about the research approach and findings. Such a summary may be one to three pages long. Longer reports (over 30 pages) may require a longer executive summary. However, an executive summary's informative value far exceeds the importance of its length; a long, informative summary detailing recommendations is more valuable than a short, unclear one.

This important section should have the heading "Executive Summary," and it may include subheadings such as "Topic and Purpose," "Findings," and "Recommendations." While the summary is the last part of the document that is written, it should be placed before the Introductory section.

Here is an example of an executive summary appropriate for the example used earlier in this chapter.

Executive Summary

Topic and Purpose

This report considers a problem with parking availability and ways to address it. A survey of students was conducted to ascertain student attitudes about the parking situation and what to do about it.

Recommendations

The University should construct a parking deck in a central location on campus. A $100 fee will be added to each student's semester bill to help fund construction and maintenance. A parking deck, funded by students, will reduce congestion around campus while making the campus appear favorable to prospective students.

As we saw in an earlier chapter, the executive summary is the only section of a report that all managers will always read. It is not clear how much of a report or proposal a given manager or executive will read; however, it is virtually guaranteed that she will read the executive summary. This section must be written in a way that allows the reader to infer the contents of the report.

Because of the conciseness of an executive summary, neuroscientific implications are limited for the most part to reward neurons (identifying specific recommendations to address a problem); mirroring values of conciseness and clarity; and allaying fear, if possible.

Presenting Information Visually: Graphics and Neuroscience

Graphics such as pie charts, bar graphs, tables, line graphs, and diagrams are popular in business reports for several reasons:

1. Conciseness: They provide a large amount of information concisely.
2. Synergy: The entire image can be more informative than showing just a few parts of the picture or data to consider at a time ("the whole is greater than the sum of the parts").

3. Eye candy: People prefer looking at an image than reading words, if the image illustrates what the words are trying to communicate—be that a point, a spatial relationship, or general concept.

If a diagram showing how a machine performs a given task is provided along with text describing that process, readers will look at the image before they look at the text; and it may be more productive to look at that image instead of the text.[2, 3, 4] Indeed, they might look ONLY at the IMAGE to try to understand the process. Numerous publications report studies finding that our brains prefer using images to understand concepts. Images are important to understanding abstract ideas and concepts and the relationship of image to text.[5, 6] This applies to qualitative information as well as quantitative information.

Arnheim (1969) was among the earliest scholars to argue for the value of images to facilitate cognition.[7] A concept or data can be shown in its entirety whereas words are processed individually, breaking up the flow of information. If the idea or concept is presented graphically for readers, it is more efficient than having the readers try to imagine it themselves. An individual may be able to better understand a concept that is represented graphically, because the brain processes the entire image toward understanding relationships within it. Arnheim's point about cognition and visual representation is that the image needs to convey meaning explicitly or link closely to the reader's prior experiences. So, the writer or designer of the image needs to consider how to link the concept to the reader's prior experiences.

Hicks (1973), Mitchell (1995), and Mayer (2001) called attention to a relationship that exists between words and images.[8, 9, 10] Text has only one way of being read, while visual forms can be read any number of ways. With the right words, the visual can perform its function better. Mayer noted that if a picture is provided, people can make the visual connection more readily.

General Principles of Integrating Visuals into Managerial Writing

One can show a process involved in manufacturing a product to help the audience understand the various stages involved in the process. A diagram can illustrate the various components of a particular product. A map can help the audience understand the relative location of a given city where a new office for a business might open and other cities and related market demographics nearby. These graphics illustrate qualitative information.

Quantitative information such as revenues, profits, and costs can be represented graphically, too. A graphic representation is ideal for such data, especially if showing trends (line graph or bar graph) or a breakdown of variables involved (bar graph or pie chart). These graphics provide a visual form of narrative related to quantitative data.

Principles related to designing and using graphics are identified by many writers. Different kinds of graphics facilitate different kinds of cognition. Table 4.1 shows different kinds of graphics and how they can best be utilized in a business document.

In addition to understanding which type of graphic to include, you must understand HOW to use graphics; avoid placing a graphic on a page or slide without engaging it well. These are tips for integration of graphics:

1. Referral: Refer to the graphic in the text, place appropriately, and discuss. Don't just place a graphic on a page without referring to it and discussing it.
   a. Examples of textual reference:
      i. "Table 4.1 shows that…" or
      ii. "… (see Table 4.1)."

Table 4.1 Uses of various graphics

Graphic	Description or purpose(s)
Table	Lists specific numeric data using rows or columns; emphasis on numbers—less on relationships.
Line graph	Shows data points on a plot graph with a line connecting data points; shows trends over time or relationships across data points.
Pie chart	Shows proportions of a whole (100 percent). Each section should look unique from any other section, and percentages should add up to 100 percent.
Map	Shows specific location of something and relation to other location points.
Diagram	Shows spatial relationships and or progression.
Organizational diagram (chart)	Shows relationships within an organization—who is responsible for whom; who reports to whom.

2. Placement: Place in the text of the report those graphics that include primary information—that is, information immediately relevant to the purpose of the report. Graphics that include secondary or tertiary information—that is, information relevant to the report but not directly relevant to the purpose of the report—should be placed in the appendix.
3. Balance: Be sure the graphic is balanced on the page, with adequate use of white space.
4. Sizing: Size the graphic appropriately so information can be read. Don't force the graphic to fit into a limited space on a page. Be sure to use enough space so information represented is clearly shown.
5. Labeling: Label all elements in a graphic appropriately. Use a legend when needed to identify colors or patterns used in the graphic. A measure of scale is helpful when using maps (example: "1 inch equals 5 feet").
6. Acknowledgment: Provide the source for all graphics if borrowed from another source.

Figure 4.1 shows effective integration of a graphic into a market study I conducted for an educational organization several years ago. The purpose of the study was to report findings of various research approaches toward addressing enrollment decline. The illustration includes both the introductory passage, setting up the graphic; the placement of the graphic; and the concise statement interpreting the data in the graphic.

In addition to the reduction in TOTAL enrollment during this period, there has been a reduction in the percentage of traditional students relative to the total population from 2010 to 2013. Figure 4 illustrates this data.

Figure 4
Traditional student enrollment as percentage of total student population (2010–2013)

2010	2011	2012	2013
51	56	48	40

While there is an increase initially, a decline occurs and drops significantly.

Figure 4.1 Effective Integration of Graphic in Report

The graphic in Figure 4.1 reports a breakdown of the pattern of student enrollment over a period of time. The graphic (Figure 4 in the report) provides a breakdown showing a trend of enrollment decline. This graphic is of primary information relative to the purpose of the report.

Notice that the graphic summarizes some findings regarding the trend. I referred to the graphic PRIOR to its placement on the same page. Finally, I offer a single sentence to capture the gist of the information in the graphic.

The following case provides application in using graphics that meet audience needs.

Case 4.1 Using Graphics Effectively

Situation

Critique the effectiveness of the design and use of the graphic Figure 4 in the example above relative to the audience considerations. The audience comprises administrators and faculty at an academic institution.

Tasks

1. What attributes of the audience can you assume?
2. How could the graphic have been formatted differently, considering the audience considerations elements (in the following list)?

Rewards:
What will motivate this person to respond a certain way (what reward can I offer?)?
How can I phrase the message so that reward is explicitly stated?

Mirroring:
What does the audience think of me (including my trustworthiness)?
What of my attributes or qualities does the audience value or admire?
How can I appeal to that perception?
What attributes or qualities of my audience do I value or admire?
How can I integrate those into my message?
What terms can I use that my audience values and will get their attention?

Fears:

What about this situation may invoke fear in my audience?

Do I want to raise fear to provide some kind of motivation toward action?

How can I defuse or minimize that fear for my audience?

To what from their experiences might my audience compare this situation, and how can I help them overcome that fear or the fear they experienced before?

3. Do you consider the graphic to be effective as is, or should it have been formatted differently? Why? If it should have been formatted differently, how?

Links to the Neuroscience Formula

Just as a graphic can represent information more concisely, you can integrate the various attributes of the formula into a graphic concisely. For example, you can activate another's reward neurons by showing a line graph that represents future growth trending upwards. Such a graph mirrors the audience's values (profit and growth). Likewise, you can elicit fear in an audience by showing a line graph that depicts profits trending downward.

Placing a downward-trending line graph in the portion of a proposal identifying a problem and why it needs to be addressed will have the particular impact the proposer wants from the audience—fear. That fear is minimized by showing the upward-trending line graph when describing the potential solution.

The following case reinforces the need for graphics and text to work together to achieve maximum impact on the audience.

Case 4.2 Making Graphics and Text Work Together

Situation

You work for a large company in your field of interest. Your company deals with customers or clients on a regular basis. A recent study by the Customer Service Department has found that with each additional representative a customer or client has to speak with about a given issue, the more frustrated that customer/client feels. Indeed, with each new person he or she has to talk to, the customer or client becomes 20 percent more frustrated about the situation generally. By the time the customer has talked to five different people, his or her frustration level has doubled.

Task

Develop a graphic showing this phenomenon, and compose a message acknowledging the phenomenon and why the company needs to address the problem. Be sure to refer to the graphic in your passage. The passage should be not more than 50 words.

CHAPTER 5

Correspondence: Communicating to Leadership Externally

While most of the chapters in this book provide cases internal to a company—communication between coworkers or people within the same organization—this chapter focuses on examples and cases with external situations. Because various office politics affect internal communication, it is much easier to illustrate the principles introduced in Chapter 2 with an external message. In this chapter, we will consider a situation that involves raising the awareness of a company's leadership about a problem with the company and requesting action on it. Application of neuroscience to messages can facilitate better communication outside of the workplace as well as within it.

Elements of Effective Claim Messages

As a private consumer or business customer or client, you often will need to communicate with someone in a company with which you are doing business. In a business setting, such situations may involve communicating with another company, such as supplier, about a problem your company is having with its processes or operations. In business communication circles, we refer to such a message as a "**claim message**." This is a message that calls attention to a problem a customer or client has with a product or service and seeks an adjustment. Among Hamm's[1] "five messages leaders must manage," this is likely to fall under those of Results: articulating weak or poor results, but framing the message as a tool to improve results; and Corporate Culture: defining standards for success.

When communicating with peers at other companies, the general expectation is that both you and they have high standards.

Such a message should include details involved in the purchase, use or application, recognition of the problem, and attempts to address it. These form the narrative of the experience. A claim message, also, may be relatively long compared to other kinds of messages because of the importance of these details. The details provide information to help the reader understand the entire experience, the related product or service, and how his own company may be responding to it. The clarity of the situation conveyed with those details is very important to helping the reader understand how to respond. One should not sacrifice clarity for conciseness.

The claim message can also include suggestions for addressing the problem, providing parameters of what the customer thinks is a reasonable response. Tact and diplomacy are also important within such messages, applying principles of reader perspective, or sensitivity to the audience's perspective. Such messages may occur via e-mail, of course; however, they may involve hard copy print exchanges as well. Though the discussion that follows includes letter formatting elements, the principles of message development apply equally to both letters and e-mail. However, a letter may bring with it a different kind of response than an e-mail.

A business letter may have a certain impact depending on how it is presented. Letterhead adds a visual attribute—a fancy design or logo—that makes the message seem more official than if a letterhead was not included. Letterhead may also include a haptic (or touch or tactile) attribute if it is raised. These elements create a rhetorical effect. A message from an attorney's office on letterhead stationery may seem a bit more intimidating than if there was no letterhead. Likewise, letterhead on a message from a hospital or doctor's office makes the message seem more official. The letterhead seems to add ethos to the message. The letterhead seems to add credibility about the attorney's, hospital's or physician's position of authority to the message.

The envelope in which the letter or document is contained can also contribute to the effect. Most people are used to receiving letters in letter-sized envelopes. We have learned through experience that a large envelope suggests that something important is inside. A letter that is delivered directly to someone's office by the mail carrier and requires the recipient's signature to verify delivery may also create a certain response from the reader or recipient that it would not have had without that element. The letter seems more official and, consequently, more important. The combination of elements associated with the message can enhance a message's effect.

Analysis of a Claim Message

In this section, we will consider an actual message I sent to the leadership team of a major insurance provider after my wife and I experienced considerable frustration resolving some problems in coordinating our employer-related insurance benefits. I discussed the situation and letter in *The Neuroscience of Multimodal Persuasive Messages,*[2] but I treat it a bit differently here. While this example is a form of a claim message from an employee or customer to a provider, consider similarities it could easily have with a message from a vice president of human resources to an insurer upon learning of problems employees are having with the company's insurer. While the vice president might omit some of the more specific details provided, he would compose a very similar message, though he might contact the insurer by phone to address the situation. Nevertheless, he would convey the problems, using a few examples of the difficulties employees are having.

While names of people and organizations involved in the situation and message have been changed (shown later in Figure 5.1) to protect the privacy of those involved, I left virtually all of the remaining details intact. As I composed the message, several attributes of neuroscience were on my mind, particularly mirror neurons, reward neurons, and plasticity. I also integrate consideration of attributes related to the hippocampus, encouraging the audience to recall past experiences.

In crafting the letter, I started with the rhetorical situation relative to the formula provided in Chapter 2. I then applied the formula within the message:

Situation--→ Desired Action or Response--→ Audience's Needs--→ Message

Situation

As I mentioned, my wife and I had experienced frustration at the inability to coordinate medical coverage between our respective employer-related benefits. Coordination of benefits occurs when multiple insurers are involved in possible coverage of members, and it is the act of contacting each insurer to indicate which insurance carrier is the primary insurance and which is secondary for billing purposes. My wife and I had insurance coverage for our family as full-time employees of our respective employers. While coverage was provided by different companies, the two companies were actually affiliated with each other. In spite of our efforts to coordinate benefits, the carriers constantly confused which was the primary and which was the secondary insurance; and we continued to receive bills for covered care.

We had made several phone calls—to both insurance companies and to billing offices—to try to correct the situation; but our efforts seemed always to fail. Our experience is detailed, for the most part, in the letter. A staff member at a billing office shared with my wife an experience she had with her family that was similar to ours. She even provided what she thought was happening to cause the errors; as someone who is experienced with billing processes, we assumed she understood what was probably happening better than we could. I decided to contact the leadership team of the main insurance carrier for several reasons: Not only was I frustrated at the amount of time it was taking to correct the issue, the companies were affiliated with each other. So, coordinating benefits between the two companies should not have been that challenging. Also, considering that our experience was not unique and the issue may be internal to the companies, I felt that the leadership team needed to be aware of the experiences involving multiple units within its entities. Management may not be aware of specific issues personnel at lower levels are having if those people are trying to address it themselves without alarming management at higher levels.

Desired Action or Response

At minimum, I wanted to be able to correct the issue that was causing the problem. Why were we still getting these bills when they should have been paid by insurance companies that are affiliated with each other? Why was there so much confusion between two affiliated companies?

Additionally, my wife and I wanted them to understand the inconveniences the situation caused us relative to time and effort. We spent a lot of time on the phone with the various people involved. We both work full time and manage a busy household. It seemed quite a bit of our valuable and scarce time was spent on the phone trying to address this issue.

Here are some issues we considered in our communication.

Audience's Needs

Rewards:

> What will motivate this person to respond a certain way (What reward can I offer?)?
> The company's reputation.
> Communicating positive outcome to a large audience of business students.

> How can I phrase the message so that reward is explicitly stated?
> Include these points in my message.

Mirroring:

> What does the audience think of me?
> They don't know who I am.

> What of my attributes or qualities does the audience value or admire?
> They do not know me, but they can research me online, and I can provide some information about my background to help them understand what they might value of my background.

> How can I appeal to that perception?
> By linking my education and leadership experience to theirs.

> What attributes or qualities of my audience do I value or admire?
> Leadership training.
> Links to my institution [several had attended my institution at one time].

How can I integrate those into my message?
Acknowledge them explicitly.

What terms can I use that my audience values and will get their attention?
Leadership-related terms.
Personal finance terms.

Fears:

What about this situation may invoke fear in my audience?
Bad reputation.
Company not matching its values or philosophies to customer experience.

Do I want to raise fear?

How can I defuse or minimize that fear for my audience?
While raising the fear in them, I can also suggest how to address it.

To what from their experiences might my audience compare this situation, and how can I help them overcome that fear or the fear they experienced before?
I can make explicit comparisons to personal experiences and to what I understand of business education.

Mode of Delivery:

How can I best deliver this message to get the desired response from my audience?
Writing—letter or e-mail? [just print-linguistic text]
Phone call? [just aural]
In person? [multimodal]

I was not able to ascertain the leadership team's e-mail or phone contact information on the company's website. The only contact information I could find there was the address of the headquarters. So, I decided to write a letter detailing the situation and problem. In business writing pedagogy parlance, the letter would be considered a claim letter.

The letter was addressed to the president of the company and was copied to several relevant vice presidents, since multiple units of the business seemed to be contributing to the problem. Had I ascertained that only one unit was involved, I would have addressed only that vice president. As such, the audience is most of the company's leadership team, and the purpose of the message is to address a problem with coordination of benefits. The excerpted message is provided in Figure 5.1. You will note a lengthy narrative; however, that narrative has a purpose—to help the readers clearly understand the experience and engage neural phenomena.

MESSAGE

1234 Some St
Anywhere, ST 34567
April xx, 20yy

Ronald Smith, Chairman, President and Chief Executive Officer
Medical Insurer Co.
Someplace

Dear Mr. Smith,
I am a customer of Medical Insurer through The University's heath care plans, and my wife is a customer of Cover You Insurer through her employer. I write to express dismay and frustration with recent experiences related to multiple patient accounts and an inability to coordinate benefits between Medical Insurer and Cover You Insurer, which are part of the same company. My wife and I have done what your customer service personnel have asked us to do in addressing bills from This Hospital and That Hospital; yet, we continue to receive past due notices and bills from these medical providers. The hospital billing staff also have acknowledged their frustrations in dealing with customers insured through the two entities. So, our case is not unique. I am writing to you in particular, because we perceive an issue with multiple units within your companies and because **our experience is counter to Medical Insurer's stated service philosophy and values.**

Figure 5.1 Example of a claim letter requesting action

In the past, I have had very good experiences with Medical Insurer as my primary insurer. However, the experiences my wife and I have had in the past year have not met with that same satisfaction. Our case has created frustration for us for the past 7 months. If it is our error, we do not know what to do to correct it; our phone calls have not worked. If it is an internal issue, there is a clear lack of communication between your companies, and the information system(s) involved is/are lacking effective coordination within it or between them. In any case, our experience has been far from Medical Insurer's service philosophy of placing the needs of the patient first.

I received a third notice of past due payment in [month] on service rendered over a year ago for my daughter. My wife and I both had coverage through our respective employer (please see the copied member cards). In previous months I received messages indicating reasons for lack of coverage; and these generally involved coordination of benefits issues, not rejection or coding errors. This issue took over 5 months to resolve…; my wife and I made several phone calls each week for about a month. I am also in the midst of dealing with a similar situation related to surgery… (see 3rd enclosure). I just received another bill related to it. In most of these cases, as with the 4th enclosure, we were told that the secondary insurer needed to know how much the primary insurer paid out. Again, the two companies are connected; so, I hope you can understand our frustration at this challenge. This should not be difficult to ascertain internally.

My wife and I have contacted the medical provider regarding each of these accounts, and they encouraged us to contact our insurance providers. My wife and I have each contacted both Medical Insurer (MI) and Cover You (CY), and each time we were told that they would follow up on the account. I have spoken on different occasions with Someone (CY), Another (CY), and More (MI). They generally take down information from both insurance accounts and say they will follow up. We have provided EOBs as well. We then contact the hospital or medical provider to encourage them to resubmit the claim.

Figure 5.1 (Continued)

Hospital billing departments know of the issues associated with coordination of benefits between the two entities. Multiple billing personnel have expressed sympathy with our situation. One, at This Hospital's billing department, acknowledged that she has experienced the same problems from other patients who have MI and CY coverage, and it has affected her own family as well. She understands that the MI and CY computer system becomes confused and automatically uses the first name it recognizes alphabetically as the primary insurer. That could explain the problem in our case as well.

If One's conclusion is accurate, the information systems between your companies need to be better developed and coordinated to facilitate better communication and categorization as primary or secondary insurer between the two entities. Again, **this experience and what we are hearing from medical providers' billing offices are contrary to Medical Insurer's service philosophy of placing the needs of the patient first.** On a personal level, I hope you can understand our frustration that the company does not seem able to coordinate with its own entities and the communication challenges we have faced as customers trying to address any errors on our part. These coordination issues may lead to our accounts going to collection, negatively affecting our personal credit. This does not create peace of mind or trust in your companies to do things right. I am confident that you and your leadership team will fight aggressively to ascertain the cause of such an issue if it affected you and them as it has us. On a professional level, I will use this example to teach business students how to address such communication issues; and I hope you will use it to help improve communication at your companies.

I teach professional writing courses at The University, and we often use case studies to facilitate analyses and reports simulating "real world" scenarios. This current dilemma is an excellent example of a series of communication-related problems affecting a business internally and externally. I recall in my own education experience a professor who provided us with information about how a specific company

Figure 5.1 (Continued)

responded to a scenario that we had just worked on as a case study. It was fascinating to compare how we suggested handling the situation with how the company actually handled it and the result. I will share your response with our students.

Finally, as a study in leadership, this case can be used to demonstrate how closely committed a leadership team is to its company's philosophies and values. I graduated from the Leadership Institute, The University's leadership development program, in 2xxx. We often discussed links between a company's values and users' or customers' experiences. When the user's or customer's experience does not match the company's values or philosophy, there is a problem.

Your company strives to create peace of mind for customers. That has not been our experience in the past several months, and it sounds like others are having similar experiences with your companies.

Thank you for considering our experience and looking into remedies for it. I look forward to your response.

Sincerely,

Dirk Remley

Enclosures (4)

xc:

Mr. X, Chief Communications Officer

Ms. Y, Chief Information Officer

Ms. Z, Chief Marketing Officer

Ms. T, Chief Customer Service Officer

Figure 5.1 *(Continued)*

Discussion

I sent each copy of the letter illustrated in Figure 5.1 to the recipients in a U.S. Postal Service Express Mail envelope. It is a little larger in size and of a heavier stock than standard paper or standard envelopes. I did not fold the paper containing the message and enclosures. The pages of the message and the enclosures were paper-clipped together inside the envelope.

As I indicated, the message is longer than most would perceive acceptable for a business message; however, it represents several months of experiences and the details are important to help the reader understand the situation. Consider, though, that the main point is conveyed in the first paragraph and the remainder of the message is the detailed explanation of it. In this respect, it applies elements of lean communication. Again, a vice president of human resources would likely omit some of the thicker details in a business-to-business message. However, the narrative helps establish the frustration we experienced, and that is important to convey. I introduce the topic and purpose in the opening paragraph—standard in any business writing situation.

I also make an immediate connection to the company's values and philosophy. This is my first integration of neuroscience, and it will appeal to the audience quickly. Leadership is always concerned about how the company is meeting its corporate mission, philosophy, and values. In some executive-level settings, presentations must begin with an explicit reference to the topic's positioning within the company's mission and philosophies; that is how important those elements are to a company's leadership. This appeal combines both pathos (emotion) and logical reasoning that is based on neural plasticity associated with leadership development. Leaders learn how to use these terms in communication, and they learn to value the concepts. I have immediately engaged a value of my audience.

In the second paragraph, I provide a "good feeling" message, referring to previous experiences with the company and offering some element of reward—success in the past. Usually, when something about us or our work is critiqued, a critique that includes some positive elements of us or our work is likely to be better-received and seem less like an attack than one in which only negative attributes of us or our work are presented. It reflects some objectivity in assessing our work, helping to establish the speaker's or assessor's own credibility. It, also, feels better knowing that we did something well. I call attention to the specific issue, again, referring explicitly to the company website. This shows that I have researched the company. There is a mirroring dynamic here. Leadership was likely involved in developing the statements. As educated professionals, they probably do quite a bit of research online themselves. I have shown that I am researching the company and reading their statements. I mirror their actions and values.

Paragraphs 3 through 5 outline our negative experiences, alluding explicitly to hospital billing departments having a problem. This suggests an issue with customer service and, possibly, communications; so those officers are paying close attention to this part of the message. This review of incidents is also a logical appeal, drawing on reward neurons of the audience. If others are experiencing and noting a problem, this is bad for the company's reputation. Consequently, an effect on the amygdala also occurs; the company leaders fear the implications of a bad reputation. Many will be aware of reports about other leaders and executives who have been fired or had to resign because of an event or operational problem that resulted in compromising the company's reputation, especially if the executive was aware of the problem and did nothing about it. The leadership team knows it will be held responsible for repercussions related to this problem. Generally, if we understand that we will be held responsible for something bad happening, to the point of losing our job, we try to address the issue quickly to eliminate or minimize the potential problem.

In paragraph 6, I acknowledge the billing department staffer's speculation about a cause, linking it to our experience as well as linking it to the company's values and philosophy. In connecting our experience to the company's values, I draw on logical and pathetic appeals based on reward neuron dynamics and plasticity of leadership's values. In leadership's experience, they have emphasized these principles internally and are used to expressing action relative to those values and philosophies. These are terms they use on a regular basis, and an outsider is calling attention to them. I am mirroring their language. Further, the staffer's speculation offers a reasonable cause. She has experienced the coordination problem with a number of patients' accounts and has observed a pattern emerge. One can draw a logical conclusion about what is happening based on such observations. It is reasonable, further, to understand that a computer system may be programmed to list names alphabetically, contributing to the problem in this situation. Consequently, the information officer understands that he may need to look into this possible issue with the information system.

Paragraphs 7 to 10 are where I actively and explicitly engage mirror neurons—facilitating connections between me and the audience. I refer to my own experiences in a leadership position; so, they understand that I, too, have "executive-level" experiences and concerns. I can empathize to some degree with them. Generally, we react differently to people who understand our own situation and concerns than we do to someone whom we understand has never experienced what we experience. The reader may understand that I am trying to help them rather than attack them. I also link my education to theirs; I learned from researching their background on the company website that all have an MBA degree, as many executive officers do. MBA education often includes case studies based on real situations. A professor may be aware of the actual action the company took and the outcome of that action and share it with his or her students. I acknowledge my experience in a leadership training program, which most of them have experienced. My message here is that I am not dramatically different from them with respect to our leadership backgrounds. I appeal to them on a personal level as well as professional; leaders are human and have a personal life. From their own experiences as a customer, they would understand the frustration such errors can cause. They understand the importance of one's credit rating; so, they can mirror and empathize with my frustration. In this sense, I switch the perspective—they can mirror me as a customer concerned about their credit rating.

In paragraph 10, I try to engage reward neurons, but I do not know how the readers will respond to it. By mentioning that I will share their response with my students, I hope that they perceive a potential reward by acting on the situation and corresponding a certain way, making them look favorable. As I note, they likely experienced that discussion in their MBA programs—hearing about how a company responded to a specific case as part of a case study follow up. If the company responded well, the students probably felt it made the company look good. As a case study, they would want students to have that same reaction; their response may help the company to look good. This would be of particular interest to the marketing officer; marketing becomes a challenge when the company's reputation is suffering.

In terms of delivery, again, I sent this as a letter. There is a multimodal effect related to spatial, tactile, and visual appearance. While I did not include letterhead, I use bold in a few paragraphs; and I sent copies of it in 9" × 12" express mail envelopes to their offices. The bold typeface integrates a visual attribute beyond "normal" typeface. That would get their attention and emphasize particular information. Also, the envelopes would stand out from other mail they may receive, taking up a bit more space than standard letter envelopes. The envelope size design also gave it a more important look than a regular envelope and feels differently than holding a standard-sized envelope.

Further, I included my business card. This draws on plasticity associated with "official" business practices and elicits mirror neurons. Sharing of business cards is a frequent practice as part of a formal introduction. I am mirroring a standard practice they are used to experiencing.

The letter may seem more important, too, coming from a large envelope that included the visual stimuli associated with the words "Express delivery" and other colorful text on the envelope's design. So, the letter is accessed just after experiencing the envelope's size, eliciting the perception of importance. Finally, the contents of the envelope involved no fewer than seven pages and a business card; it feels thick. I did not use the larger envelope just to create a rhetorical effect; it would have been impractical to try to fold all of the pages involved into a standard letter mailing envelope. The thickness of the message packet may also create the perception of importance relative to the visual and tactile attributes associated with size.

So, it may have been better to send this message as a letter than as an e-mail. Consider that an e-mail of the same message would have included a number of attachments that may or may not have been delivered well because of technological issues, and the message may not have seemed as important as just another e-mail message.

Result

About a week after sending the message, I received a phone call from someone who introduced herself as the president's assistant. She acknowledged that the leadership team had received the letter and had talked about it at some length. The president gave it to her and asked her to pursue the situation.

Over the course of several weeks, the situation was corrected, and the assistant encouraged us to continue to contact her directly to address future similar billing issues. Eventually, I received a letter from one of the VPs, in which he indicated new steps the company was taking to assure such a situation would not happen again. We successfully attained our desired result.

Even as we received new bills for services other than those mentioned in the letter, we maintained contact with the assistant to address any bill we perceived to have not been properly handled, and she responded to each situation directly. The president's assistant had become our direct contact within the company.

Conclusion

What seems to be an entirely "print" business document or message was, actually, multimodal, depending on certain attributes of the format of the message as well as the media associated with delivery. The rhetorical effectiveness of these messages can be affected by decisions regarding such format and delivery features.

Case 5.1 provides an opportunity for your response in regard to another, similar situation, also based on a personal experience. I change details of the situation to develop a workplace-related case.

Case 5.1 Dissatisfied Customer Seeks Adjustment

Background

The case involves an exchange between your company and a supplier. You are to consider a response that applies the concepts we have discussed. Write out a response; then, compare it to my response. As you review my response (which, admittedly, is among the harshest I have ever composed), locate where I apply the concepts and what I may be trying to accomplish with each. Remember the formula as you compose your response:

Situation--→ Desired Action or Response--→ Audience's Needs--→ Me--→ Message

Situation

Assume that you and your organization want to update a few rooms in the building you occupy. One of these updates involves redesigning a room to facilitate a meeting space that can be used for executive meetings as well as social gatherings involving food and beverages. The room also can be used when recruiting new executives. The redesign includes a counter top and sink as well as a backsplash. You and two others on your team have visited a couple of home improvement stores as you considered material, appearance, and price. After a few weeks of shopping around, you decide on a particular counter top and backsplash, both from the same store. You go in to the store on a Saturday morning, figuring the purchase process will take not more than 30 minutes since you know what you were purchasing. The store is offering an incentive to purchase counter tops by a certain date for installation to occur by a certain holiday, and you find the incentive and timing very appealing; the company has a holiday party scheduled, and this would be a great opportunity to show off the new space, especially with two executive searches going on.

The sales associate is serving another customer as you arrive in the kitchen counter top department. The customer, however, is not with the sales associate, but instead is looking at different items in the department, shopping, and comparing items before making a decision. The sales associate asks you to wait since she is busy with the other customer and she is the only kitchen associate working at the time. She acknowledges that another associate is expected in about an hour. As you wait for her, you walk around to locate another associate who may be able to help you. The associates hesitate to help, not knowing procedures in the kitchen counter top department. You continue to wait, noting that the associate is not directly helping the other customer. Eventually, after about 10 minutes, you ask again for her help; and she reluctantly takes you to a table to begin the purchase process.

The computer is very slow, and it takes several minutes to input the order specifics. The associate continues to look for the other customer as she tries to input the order details. You feel pressed for time, as you have other plans for spending your Saturday. You begin to wonder whether you should just leave and return another day or go to the other home improvement store, which is a very short drive away. You decide to stay, even as the delay continues and the associate indicates a desire to help the other customer who is now ready for her help. Eventually, the purchase order is made and you pay for it; however, the associate does not talk you through the process and forgets to ask you about financing and other important items. Indeed, because of the slow computers and being pressed for time, you leave without the paperwork.

Part of the purchase process involves having someone come to the office to measure the counter area to create a template. This occurs within a reasonable timeframe after the purchase (within 2 weeks), and you wait to hear from the store about scheduling installation. You purchase the backsplash with a different sales associate, and that purchase goes much more smoothly. The backsplash measurement person comes out just before the counter top person; so a timely installation of both looks promising.

You have not heard from the store for a few weeks; not knowing how long it normally takes them to get everything in order, you initially do not call to ask. Becoming concerned after almost a month, you call to ask about the installation. You are told there is no paperwork related to the purchase or the templator's visit. Only after you explain what you had purchased and your experience, the person with whom you are speaking finds the paperwork and says she will call you back after looking into some issues. The store, evidently, has misplaced or lost your paperwork!

Apologetic, the store manager contacts you and offers a gesture of goodwill—a discount on the purchase price. You feel this is reasonable, and you move forward with scheduling the work for the tear out of the old counter top and installations. As you work to set a schedule for installation, you talk to three different "project managers," all of whom seemed not to know much about the project. You have to describe the situation and your experience with each one. You understand that the counter installation will occur before the backsplash work. Details are eventually worked out and installation occurs.

Desired Action

Considering all of the inconveniences and delays that you experienced, you want to make sure the executives of the home improvement store know what had happened. You were poorly treated and experienced a few episodes of unprofessional behaviors. You want some kind of compensation, given all the time you spent on the phone and related frustrations in getting the work coordinated and done. You also can suggest some changes based on your experience.

Tasks

1. You are writing via e-mail to the store chain's chief operations officer. Complete the audience analysis questionnaire before beginning your message:

   Rewards:
   What will motivate this person to respond a certain way (What reward can I offer?)?
   How can I phrase the message so that reward is explicitly stated?

   Mirroring:
   What does the audience think of me?
   What of my attributes or qualities does the audience value or admire?
   How can I appeal to that perception?
   What attributes or qualities of my audience do I value or admire?
   How can I integrate those into my message?
   What terms can I use that my audience values and will get their attention?

   Fears:
   What about this situation may invoke fear in my audience?
   How can I defuse or minimize that fear for my audience?

To what from their experiences might my audience compare this situation, and how can I help them overcome that fear or the fear they experienced before?

Mode of Delivery:

How can I best deliver this message to get the desired response from my audience?

Writing—letter or e-mail? [just print-linguistic text]

Phone call? [just aural]

In person? [multimodal]

2. Develop a response that includes a review of the situation, the desired response, and two or three recommendations for improving the customer experience.

Figure 5.2 is a variation of the letter that I wrote to the chief operations officer of the home improvement store. I have changed the details pertaining to the personal experience toward applying details of the case study above. My letter brought a similar result as that of the example earlier in this chapter.

Dear Mr. Dude,

I write to report on a very unpleasant experience with your store number 456 (City) and what my company and I feel is an unacceptable response to the various problems we have had with our purchase of a countertop and backsplash to replace existing counter top and backsplash in our office space. The experience reflects several problems with store operations, including customer service. Between the "bum's rush" I was treated to from the sales associate to the store losing the templator's form and confusion about the process and related delays, I feel as if I have been treated very poorly by several people at the store. When I purchased the items in mid September, I was promised the installation would occur by Holiday; but that did not occur because of MUCH miscommunication between X Co. and us and X Co. and the

Figure 5.2 Example of claim letter seeking adjustment

installers. We are also having to pay more than what we thought for services we were not made aware were in addition to the basic order.

Having gone to the store and a nearby Different Company a couple of times to look at countertops and ascertain which we wanted, on [date], I went to store 456 to purchase the counter top and related backsplash items. My company and I felt it was the best deal and were excited that promotional material promised installation by Holiday. We had not used X Co. for installation, but we had purchased from it several times before this.

I was delayed in speaking to the sales associate, [name], as she was helping another customer. She was the only associate in the area who could help us, the store being shorthanded that day (a Saturday morning). After several delays, and in a hurry to get back home, we asked with some anxiousness to place the order. [Associate], then, assisted us with the order. [Associate] acknowledged that, technically, she wasn't the countertop person; that she was standing in for the countertop associates, one of whom was on vacation and the other who was to come in later that day.

The computer was very slow, and [Associate] seemed very rushed to get back to another customer. The order took a long time to place—not less than 20 minutes. [Associate] was still anxious to return to the other customer and forgot to ask us about financing options and to detail the installation process. Consequently, I did not know that we were to find someone else to tear out the existing counter top and disconnect the related plumbing and stove top. I left the store without paperwork for the $[xxxx] order, the computers being too slow and [Associate] in a hurry to return to her customer. The paperwork was e-mailed to us later the next week.

On [date], we purchased the backsplash from [Associate 2]. We also purchased some ceramic flooring for a bathroom project from her, and in both cases, she explained the estimation and installation processes and made us aware of everything involved. The ceramic flooring has been installed, and we are happy with it.

Figure 5.2 (Continued)

Also, in early [month], the backsplash installer came to estimate the work and indicated that the countertop needed to be installed before the backsplash could be installed. This is important, because the entire process or project is delayed because of the countertop issues. Within a week of that visit, the countertop estimator or templator came to review specifics for that installation. He filed his report; but we did not hear anything from X Co.

A few weeks later, my associate called X Co. and asked about progress. She was first told that the store had no record of any such paperwork. When pressed, they found the filed paperwork and began the process to set up the installation. [Name] is among three project managers we have spoken with from the store, none of whom seem to talk to each other, as suggested by the lack of information any have about the most recent conversation we've had with others. I have spoken with [store manager], store manager, and [store associate manager], the associate store manager. **The lack of communication among store administrators is very frustrating, contributing to general miscommunication.** When we have called and had our calls forwarded to another department the call often is dropped, even when we are on a landline. **This is very frustrating as well; is the employee dropping the call because they don't want to talk to me? Or does the employee not know how to transfer the call accurately?**

My associate talked with [store manager], the store manager, several times in an effort to understand what was happening and to coordinate the work. [store manager] provided compensation in the form of a percentage discount related to the store losing the filed paperwork and forgetting about us. After coordinating schedules with everyone involved, we set plans for the installation to occur the weekend before [Holiday], with the counter top work being done on Friday of that weekend. Recognizing that we might be without a counter top in time to prepare Holiday festivities, we decided to arrange for a restaurant party. **The delay related to the lost paperwork caused us to have to spend more money.**

Figure 5.2 (Continued)

It took 3½ months for the installation to occur, and we missed opportunities to use the space for an office party and for other important business activities. Given our experience with X Co., we would appreciate it if you could give us a discount of 50 percent for the inconveniences, additional expenses, and frustrations we have experienced because of X Co's actions and inactions.

Knowing you want to avoid similar negative customer experiences, I recommend that you find a way to facilitate better communication among store administrators and sales associates so that other customers do not experience the frustrations, delays, and additional expenses we have with this project. I urge you to find a way to schedule associates so someone is available to take a customer's order, even if someone from another nearby department can help. I almost walked out and went to the Home Improvement Place next door. At this point, we wish we would have.

Personally, I am confident that you would not tolerate such an experience as a customer of any home improvement store. Professionally, I know that leadership needs to hear from customers about the customer experience. I hope this input will help you to improve store operations.

Figure 5.2 (Continued)

CHAPTER 6

Correspondence: Communicating Information to New Employees

When a new employee is hired into a unit, someone often is asked to introduce the newcomer to the nature of the work in that unit as well as the work expected. This provides an orientation for the new employee. Much of this message is informational, but to some degree it is persuasive. The company is trying to persuade the new hire to "buy into" the culture of the unit or company. The employee conveyed interest in working for the company through the job application, of course; but what does he understand of the company's culture and practices? Not much, until he starts working.

The Welcome Message

Consequently, the "welcome" message needs to be inviting while informative, considering the audience's neuroscience. The new employee is curious, and to some degree fearful, but he wants to be able to make the transition to working there easily. The situation lends itself to three or four of Hamm's (2013) "Five Messages Leaders Must Manage:" "Corporate culture," "organizational hierarchy," and "time management." It can also involve conveying parameters of "your job."

Let's consider an example of such a message that is based on an experience I had coordinating a course. In it I welcome faculty who are new to teaching the course while introducing some changes from teaching approaches that they are used to experiencing.

Again, we will apply the formula:

Situation--→ Desired Action or Response --→ Audience's Needs--→ Message

Situation

As I indicated before, I have coordinated a business writing course that is required of all business majors at my institution. This coordination has involved course development, including any modifications to the course, training and mentoring any who teach the course, and acting as a liaison between the Department of English (ENG) and the Business College (BC). The liaison role has included working with someone who has coordinated an oral communication course housed in the BC as well as communicating with BC leadership. The two courses have represented communication-specific coursework in the business program. Over time, a number of assignments were explicitly linked between the two courses. At one point, there was only one explicit link between the two courses—a final report assignment; students produce a document—usually a proposal—for the ENG course and they present their findings orally in the BC course.

Administrators and faculty in the BC generally respect my background, but they prefer a different kind of approach to teaching courses than is identified as "best practice" in rhetoric and writing studies scholarship. For example, a difference that stands out is that BC wanted all sections of a given course to include the exact same content, assignments, activities, and instructional materials. Scholarship in writing studies encourages faculty to have autonomy so they can customize some material and activities for their own teaching style and student needs.

As coordinator for the course, I have been tasked with finding a balance between these approaches. Several exchanges with BC's representatives over several years involved negotiating between the two approaches. I mentioned before that the team of instructors who would teach the different sections of the course changes from semester to semester; some may have been new to the course while others were veterans.

In introducing faculty new to the course to the standardized pedagogy, I am introducing something that most have not yet experienced. They are used to having some degree of autonomy with their course. While the course objectives are the same for all sections of a writing course, individual faculty have flexibility to facilitate that learning as they feel best suits their teaching approach and with content they feel will benefit students.

Desired Action or Response

I want the audience to feel invited to the course while accepting the standardization required. Also, I want them to feel that the transition to the course will be easy, addressing a fear that many have about teaching a course for the first time. In this respect, I am persuading them to believe that it is easy.

Audience's Needs

Rewards:

What will motivate this person to respond a certain way (What reward can I offer?)?

Feeling comfortable about new course and transition to teaching it.

How can I phrase the message so that reward is explicitly stated?

Include these points in my message.

Mirroring:

What does the audience think of me?

Some know who I am, and others do not. It is my understanding that all have heard of me and a bit about me.

What of my attributes or qualities does the audience value or admire?

They do not know me, but they can research me online, and I can provide some information about my background to help them understand what they might value of my background.

How can I appeal to that perception?

By linking my education and leadership experience to their desire to teach the course with a smooth transition to it.

What attributes or qualities of my audience do I value or admire?
I don't know much about most new faculty beyond what I hear about them from others.
Willingness to teach the course; willingness to teach a course new to them.

How can I integrate those into my message?
Acknowledge them.

What terms can I use that my audience values and will get their attention?
Terms associated with writing pedagogy.

Fears:

What about this situation may invoke fear in my audience?
New course; never taught it before; don't know what to expect; don't know what to teach for a business writing course.

Do I want to raise fear?

How can I defuse or minimize that fear for my audience?
I will not acknowledge the fear explicitly, but I can also explain the support they will receive.
Also, some faculty new to a course like having the content and pedagogy set up for them. So, I can explicitly refer to the standardized approach.

To what from their experiences might my audience compare this situation, and how can I help them overcome that fear or the fear they experienced before?
It is new, but they will have lots of support. They may compare it to learning to ride a bicycle or similar; it was a struggle at first, but they knew they had a lot of support to help make that transition.

Mode of Delivery:
How can I best deliver this message to get the desired response from my audience?
Writing—letter or e-mail? [just print-linguistic text]

The first contact is always via e-mail, just out of necessity; they may not be on campus when I am.

Also, they can see that others are new as well. It can be calming to see that they are not the only ones who are new.

However, I am also asking in the message to meet with them in person, even suggesting video conferencing. I want to talk directly to them, especially if they are not acquainted with me. I do not know what they have heard of me, if anything; and I can allay some of their fears about the course and its pedagogy with my tone and facial expression. My tone and facial expression will enable me to present the verbal information with a sense of understanding, reassurance and sympathy. These are important to facilitate that smooth and easy transition to teaching the course.

Message

I am the course coordinator for [course number], and I am aware that you have been scheduled to teach at least one section of the course for the first time in the Spring 2xxx semester. I am writing to ask if you would be able to meet with me before the end of this semester to discuss the course generally and expectations to help you transition to teaching the course.

Unlike most courses you have taught, there are several parameters associated with the course consistency across sections and standardization linked to the Business College's (BC) needs. The course serves Business majors, and BC had considerable input in its development. If you have taught [course a] or [b], you are familiar with most of the content; however, BC wants us to emphasize particular content in certain ways.

The content and approach differ from those of [course b] in several ways, and I need to make you aware of those. We use a standard syllabus and course schedule, including several common assignments. Also, we do not use a textbook for the course; instructors use materials from the Resource Center to facilitate instruction and learning. There is SOME room for individualization of pedagogy, and I'll discuss these dynamics in more detail with you.

Those who teach the course also participate in a mentoring program that I facilitate throughout the semester. I try to schedule these meetings considering others' availability. We tend to meet every other week for an hour each time and discuss various issues with the course as well as some scholarship in business writing pedagogy. For many who teach the course, this is the most formal education or training they receive in business writing pedagogy. I can discuss these with you in more detail during that orientation meeting.

My office hours this semester are on [days or times]. Please let me know if any of these days or times is convenient to meet with me. I can also be on campus on [another weekday] morning if needed. During exam week, I can be available almost any morning. The sooner I can meet with you, the more time you will have to prepare for your class section(s).

I look forward to discussing the course with you and helping you transition to teaching [the course].

Discussion

There are six paragraphs, which seems to violate principles of lean communication; however, the substance of the message is conveyed in the first two paragraphs. I begin the message to new instructors with an informal introduction of myself, similar to any form of external—introducing oneself in the context of the message and acknowledging the purpose of the message. In the second paragraph, I describe some specific differences between the course and other professional writing courses they may have taught (most who teach the course have taught another professional writing course previously). This is to make the reader aware of some differences while, immediately, reassuring them of a relationship to previous experiences (hippocampus-related connection). They can recall that course and feel a bit more comfortable knowing they have experience with the general content and related pedagogy, especially in the form of activities or assignments.

I move on to detail differences further while conveying how the transition will be easy for them; the content and pedagogy are already available to them. Again, this addresses a fear for many people who teach a course for the first time. I also acknowledge the mentoring program that we use, which is for all instructors teaching the course, not just those who are new to teaching it. I acknowledge that it represents formal education in business writing pedagogy, which will reassure them further. Generally, when someone teaches one of the other professional writing courses, they will ask for tips and a syllabus to use to help them transition to the course. They receive no formal training.

I close by inviting them to let me know when we can meet, suggesting my own flexibility. Again, willingness to speak directly with them and conveying willingness to work with their schedule can put them at ease while showing support.

A few words about that face-to-face meeting: Generally, I dress professionally when I am on campus—a suit and tie or sport coat, dress shirt, dress pants, and tie. Sometimes I will go without the tie. Rarely am I dressed less formally than "business casual." So, they will understand me to be professional in my demeanor.

Humor and Sarcasm

I have a sense of humor, which I use liberally and try to place well. Humor, when used well, tends to put people at ease while facilitating important information. Most people value humor, and using it in a measured way mirrors that valuing of humor. However, humor is very difficult to convey with just print. Consequently, it is better presented in a face-to-face setting or via phone. Avoid sarcastic humor at all times, except in person with someone who will understand it. Here is a story that illustrates this problem.

Once upon a time, I drafted a proposal for a workshop at a major national conference at which I would be a cofacilitator. The other person provided feedback as I drafted the proposal. I drafted the proposal in the conference organizers' online proposal submission system. I was able to save the proposal as I revised, with the understanding that the last draft that was in the system at the submission deadline would be the version used to make a decision. The conference is competitive in that it tends to accept about one third of proposals submitted.

Colleagues in a professional organization affiliated with the conference and to which my cofacilitator and I both belonged also drafted a proposal on a topic somewhat similar to ours. They routinely facilitated a professional development workshop at the conference; so, it was generally assumed theirs would be accepted. I knew some of the people involved in that workshop, but I did not know the person drafting their proposal. They invited us to join their group of facilitators, and we eventually agreed to join them.

When word of proposal acceptance came, there was some confusion over which proposal was accepted. At first, I was confident it was their proposal, as I was sure that I deleted the draft I had in the system. My colleague with whom I drafted our initial proposal observed that our title was listed, not the organization's title; so, I asked the conference organizers to clarify which was accepted. They indicated the acceptance message pertained to the one I had "submitted." Because of the lengthy discussion dynamics involved in deciding to join the group prior to the submission deadline as well as the grading responsibilities at the time the proposal was due, I had forgotten to delete the proposal.

For a few days, I panicked at the thought of helping to facilitate at two workshops, still presuming the other would be accepted. However, early the next week, the person who drafted the organization's proposal acknowledged that the organization's proposal had been rejected. Stunned that my *draft proposal* was accepted, and embarrassed about forgetting to delete it, I apologized profusely via e-mail to the person from the professional association who developed the group proposal. She responded with acknowledgment of some dynamics of that proposal's development and included a statement to the effect that she could "blame" me for the organization's proposal not being accepted, including some phrasing declining my offer that some of them could work with our workshop. This invoked some degree of fear in me, as it reinforced my initial perception (and concern) that I was "messing up" the organization's efforts and had become a competitor. Later that same day, she wrote, asking if I "got [the] teasing tone" in her message, twice apologizing and expressing hope that I was not offended by or upset with her response, confessing her concern about potential confusion about sarcasm or her teasing tone in e-mail, and inviting me to become more involved in the organization's leadership.

Unless the audience knows you and your sense of humor, sarcasm may only worsen a situation, necessitating more time and effort to correct or clarify it. Either avoid using sarcasm in print-only settings, or make sure you express explicitly immediately after your statement that it is sarcasm.

Case 6.1 Welcoming Messages for New Employees

Situation

As we have seen, every organization has a process for welcoming new employees. Assume you are a team leader in your organization (or one you hope to work for) and have been asked to take the lead in welcoming new employees to your unit. Before composing your welcome message, consider the Audience Consideration questions as you plan the message:

Rewards:

What will motivate this person to respond a certain way (What reward can I offer?)?

How can I phrase the message so that reward is explicitly stated?

Mirroring:

What does the audience think of me (including my trustworthiness)?

What of my attributes or qualities does the audience value or admire?

How can I appeal to that perception?

What attributes or qualities of my audience do I value or admire?

How can I integrate those into my message?

What terms can I use that my audience values and will get their attention?

Fears:

In what ways might the audience fear this situation?

Do I want to raise fear to provide some kind of motivation toward action?

How can I defuse or minimize that fear for my audience?

Based on their experiences, to what might my audience compare this situation, and how can I help them overcome that fear or the fear they experienced before?

Mode of Delivery:

How can I best deliver this message to get the desired response from my audience?

Writing—letter or e-mail? [just print-linguistic text]

Phone call? [just aural]

In person? [multimodal]

Task

Compose a welcome message suitable for sending via e-mail to a new employee in your organization, department, unit, or team.

CHAPTER 7

Communicating Change to Your Team

In this chapter, we will consider two communication scenarios involving the communication of change to the team you lead. Change can be intimidating and is often met with resistance. Carefully crafted communication, however, can be useful in overcoming push back and gaining support from those we supervise. These leader-team examples will illustrate the application of our formula:

Situation--→ Desired Action or Response--→ Audience's Needs--→ Message

Framing Change

While the examples in this chapter are particular to the academic environment, they are applicable in communicating change in any organization. While it is "easy" to just issue directives for implementation, the way such directives and initiatives are presented to your team can affect their acceptance of the new policies or changes, willingness to implement them with sincerity and using reasonable effort to work with them. This would be my extension of what Hamm[1] refers to as "Organizational Hierarchy" among his "five messages leaders must manage." This type of message involves communicating change while framing it in a positive way.

As in the previous chapter, I will detail a case, illustrating the application. Then, I will challenge you to apply the formula for practice.

Situation

As I described previously, I have coordinated a business writing course that is required of all business majors at my institution. This coordination has involved course development, including any modifications to the course, training and mentoring any who teach the course, and acting as a liaison between the Department of English (ENG) and the Business College (BC). Refer to Chapter 6 for details on the course and how it has been administered.

As I indicated, the people in the BC with whom I communicate generally respect my background, but they prefer a different kind of approach to teaching courses than is identified as "best practice" in rhetoric scholarship. As coordinator for the course, I have been tasked with finding a balance between these approaches. Several exchanges with BC's representatives over several years have involved negotiating between the two approaches. Once we come to an agreement of sorts, I communicate it to those who teach the writing course. Changes to the courses have occurred over several semesters, and changes usually develop out of students' concerns over some confusion or perceptions.

I provide an excerpt of a message that I e-mailed to my "team" in which I report on some changes to the approach for teaching the course. The nature of the message is not unique, necessarily, to any one situation. To reflect that, I have removed some details (shown by ellipses and place holder labels) about the specific situation that brought about the message. However, the message reflects the kind of phrasing needed with such changes, given the standardized approach to the course.

Desired Action

I want my team to understand why the changes and updates are needed, and I want them not to fear possible issues with some of the changes. I know they will have a concern and push back against at least one update, but I can help them make that change.

Audience's Needs

Rewards:

> What will motivate this person to respond a certain way (what reward can I offer?)?
> The class will run smoothly, and there is more support.

How can I phrase the message so that reward is explicitly stated?
> Include these points in my message.

Mirroring:

What does the audience think of me?
> They respect my background and position.

What of my attributes or qualities does the audience value or admire?
> They know of my work and scholarship. They also know of my experience with BC.

How can I appeal to that perception?
> By linking my education and leadership experience to what I know they know of me, reinforcing it.

What attributes or qualities of my audience do I value or admire?
> Desire to learn some elements of course administration and working with a college of business.
> Background in business setting.

How can I integrate those into my message?
> Acknowledge them explicitly.

What terms can I use that my audience values and will get their attention?
> Terms commonly used in scholarship and BC's accreditation.

Fears:

What about this situation may invoke fear in my audience?
> Loss of autonomy—means they may not be able to address specific issues with their own section or students.

Do I want to raise fear?

How can I defuse or minimize that fear for my audience?
> While acknowledging the fear in them, I can also point out that the changes represent a small change; much of the course is already standardized.

To what from their experiences might my audience compare this situation, and how can I help them overcome that fear or the fear they experienced before?

I can make explicit comparisons to the course as they have already experienced it.

I can suggest some forms of autonomy within the new approach.

Delivery: While I communicate the message via e-mail, my goal is to have an in-person meeting.

Message

When can we meet as a group to discuss changes to the course for [x] semester?

Susan and I have discussed a few changes to both courses (mostly the BC course, but two that impact the ENG course). The xxx assignment will change, and it sounds like the yyy assignment will be modified either to be shortened or no longer be a team assignment. ... However, I hesitate to get rid of the collaborative writing assignment, because.... We may be able to reformat that assignment to include .... I don't know if we should integrate another, new assignment; because students are complaining that there's too much "work" between the two courses. I'd like your input.

Also, Susan and I have discussed using two different "templates" for the xxx assignment—one for BC and another for ENG. This will give students practice with two different templates, also reinforcing that preferred format or templates differ across companies. The file attached is the one BUS will use since it explicitly sets up a presentation (one of the ENG instructors has used it in her class), and we'll continue to use the one provided with the assignment that encourages students to outline their plans....

...To assure further "syncing" [between the two courses] the course will involve a bit less instructor autonomy relative to activities or assignments...; but I want to discuss some autonomous activities that we can integrate during the two to three work shopping weeks near the end of the semester. Also, I'm hoping to give instructors a voice in which scenarios we use for some exercises and assignments and creating such scenarios.

I want to be able to discuss all of this with you soon as a group. It represents a shift in our approach, but it is not a dramatic shift.

We have three new instructors coming on board; so, this won't be difficult for them, but we veterans are having to adjust a bit.

Please let me know if we can meet for this purpose either just prior to the [next] mentoring meeting or just afterward.

Analyzing Change Communication

Most of the application of neuroscience concepts involves application of reward neurons, mirror neurons and alleviating fear. A large fear for the faculty is that they will lose autonomy. As with any change, there is a fear of the unknown. However, there is also fear that students' learning experience will be compromised without instructor autonomy.

In the message, I make several references to the group and getting their input. This is very important in managerial communication generally—inviting input from others so they feel invested in the project or effort. However, it also stimulates reward neurons and mirror neurons. Having a voice in decisions facilitates mirroring of leadership or management. While not making the "final" decision, they are involved in the decision-making function and can influence that "final" decision. Also, they may feel a sense of reward or motivation for participating in that, not participating could mean the "final" decision involves something they don't want. They are then motivated to participate by that fear of something unappealing happening.

Also among the fears is losing a group assignment. Scholarship in managerial or business writing pedagogy encourages team activities, since so much occurs in team settings in the workplace. The group assignment in the BC course involves a very different kind of collaborative task; so, the fear is that students would lose the experience featured in the ENG course. In my message, I integrate mirroring elements, using terms my team members will understand and value. I also, acknowledge my desire to maintain the group assignment, which my team will value; I am mirroring their values. Please note, this is all very much genuine; I am not being artificial with these values and statements.

Reward and mirror neurons are also stimulated for the individual who has used the other template. My statement recognizes that she has been using something the BC coordinator values and wants to use with her students, and it recognizes her initiative in using a template that is different from that used by most of the ENG instructors. Thus, she is mirroring some "risk" assumed by management.

Now it is your turn to apply the principles we have discussed concerning change communication. The following case involves introducing a set of updates or changes to a workplace policy.

Case 7.1 Articulating Change Based on Negative Feedback

Background

Recall the situation from Chapter 5 involving the office improvement project. While you were in the position of the customer in Chapter 5, place yourself now in the position of the store manager for this chapter's activity. You have learned that a customer had a bad experience with your store involving several communication-related issues at different points in their experience.

Situation

Refer back to Chapter 5 for the details of the situation that resulted in the customer sending your company the claim letter.

As the store manager, after reviewing various procedures that affected the experience and getting input from the store's three assistant managers, you have developed new protocol for the store. These include the following changes that affect sales associates:

1. Associates will be trained to input orders related to departments near their own; this facilitates ease of movement across departments when staffing in one department is low and associates in a nearby department are not as busy. This will enable associates to help customers more effectively rather than making the customer wait or having associates feel rushed.
2. Associates are to use this new approach for customer benefit, not to compete for sales.
3. Information Technology staff will create a new system that store management can use to input customer concerns about their

experiences so that anyone in the store's upper management—manager and assistant managers—can access that information. This will expedite communication with customers and with other managers. Management can, then, communicate any discipline or training—related actions to associates.

Task

1. Decide how to communicate these changes to the sales staff. Better customer service experience is your main concern; however, the desired result with this message is that the sales staff readily accepts the new procedures and policies. Use the following considerations to guide development of the message.

Desired Result:

Audience's Needs:

Rewards:
What will motivate this person to respond a certain way (What reward can I offer?)?
How can I phrase the message so that reward is explicitly stated?

Mirroring:
What does the audience think of me?
What of my attributes or qualities does the audience value or admire?
How can I appeal to that perception?
What attributes or qualities of my audience do I value or admire?
How can I integrate those into my message?
What terms can I use that my audience values and will get their attention?

Fears:
What about this situation may invoke fear in my audience?

[Consider potential competition for sales and related commissions; how will these be addressed? This change could create a competitive environment that leads to even more customer service experience problems with associates fighting for a customer.]

Do I want to raise fear?
How can I defuse or minimize that fear for my audience?

To what from their experiences might my audience com pare this situation, and how can I help them overcome that fear or the fear they experienced before?

Delivery:
E-mail? In Person?

2. Develop a one-page rational as to how to best present this change information to employees. Include information about the message design and the mode of delivery.

CHAPTER 8

Instructional Messages: Training Manuals and Instructions

Instructional manuals tend to be considered outside of the content of managerial communication. However, training materials, including manuals and hands-on training programs, are a vital form of managerial communication. Not only do they help employees understand how to perform particular tasks, they also facilitate uniformity in performance, assuring efficiencies. I wrote about a number of dynamics related to cognition of instructional materials, especially those that involved more than just print-linguistic text, in *How the Brain Processes Multimodal Instructions*.[1] In this chapter we will focus on instructions in the form of manuals that will likely include graphics. The same principles identified in Chapter 4 regarding graphics apply here, but a few new concepts come into play because of the purpose associated with such materials—learning how to do something.

We will consider an overview of the relevant scholarship, followed by illustrations of the concepts as applied to the general formula. The overview captures the essence of one particular chapter from *How the Brain Processes Multimodal Instructions*.

Generally, studies find that the best way to approach training involves both reading and hands-on performance.[2, 3, 4, 5] People learn best when they can read information about the task, especially information that includes detailed graphics, and then are shown how to do the task and given opportunities to do it themselves.

Visual-Auditory Links

Moreno and Mayer concluded that students who received "sequential presentations" (presentations that involved reading textual information followed by animation of the process) performed best (more creative solutions) on knowledge-transfer tests.[6] Moreno and Mayer's work with these experiments is considered seminal in multimodal or multimedia instructional theory. From their experiments, they formulated some principles of multimedia instruction; some of them are included in the formula, particularly principles associated with visual dominance and an understanding of the audience's prior experiences.

The Rhetoric of Hands-On Learning and Manuals

Experiential learning, which encourages students to learn skills through performance of them—hands-on training in workplace terminology, has increased in popularity as a part of the educational experience. Internships, of course, have been valued for some time among business students and professionals. These involve much less reading and lecture-related instruction in the classroom and more practice with "real" tasks in an environment. Such a philosophy recognizes that cognition occurs by doing the task rather than by merely reading about it.

A debate ensued in the 1980s about the use of comprehensive manuals versus what was called a "minimalist manual," which limits information to the particular steps involved and omits background and theoretical information. Generally, the various studies find that the "minimalist manual" facilitates more efficient learning progress than a self-instruction manual, which offers much more background information. A study compared performance relative to the two different kinds of manuals. That study found that participants using the minimalist manual were better able to complete the tasks more quickly and with more success than those using the self-instruction manual.[7] In all cases the group that learned by doing the tasks performed better than the group that learned the tasks by reading the more extensive book about the activity. The researchers found that, while people may learn more of a task by doing it, they tend also to take *more time to perform it and have more errors* than those who learn "by the book." Using only the hands-on approach, apparently, is not an efficient approach.

Steven Pinker (1997) acknowledged that the mind works as a system that includes one's prior experiences and various forms of representation to understand information.[8] Kalyuga (2005) found that learners who had some prior experience with a task similar to what they were trying to learn were able to learn a new task more quickly than those who had no prior experience with that task.[9] This finding suggests that a manual should include an understanding of the reader's prior experiences with and knowledge about a given task so as to customize the instruction accordingly. Further, Mayer[10] and Gee[11] connected prior experience and knowledge to learning. These reinforce the role of the hippocampus, relative to memory based on experiences, and prefrontal cortex, in terms of prioritizing information and attention.

Development of Manuals

While many training programs involve shadowing and oral explanation of tasks, training manuals facilitate efficient instruction. As indicated above, a combination of reading and hands-on learning proved more efficient that just reading or just hands-on work. Many of my business students select the topic of a training manual or a training program as their final project in professional writing courses. These students have worked in various jobs—from server to management, and they explain that their training entailed 1 day to 1 week of shadowing, and that was it. Depending on the number of responsibilities they had and their complexity, they had many questions after that period; yet, they were expected to be able to do their job well. Even though it seemed efficient at the time—why waste the trainer's time or the trainee's time going over reading material—the trainees genuinely needed the reading material to understand their job better.

These students develop a manual, because they could have used one as a reference tool to help understand details of the job and related tasks. They would not have had to ask as many questions of others, delaying the work of those others or delaying their own work while waiting for the other person to respond and help.

Training manuals generally include the following sections:

Introduction: identifying task or position, and specific audience

Overview: generally describing what the task (or the position, if covering the entire position) is and what is happening

Background of the task or job or position: what is involved/tools to use/dos/don'ts

Instructions (or separate sections for each responsibility if covering entire position)

Organizational chart: showing hierarchy so person understands whom he or she should contact for questions about concerns

Directory: facilitating communication

Good instructions are essential to the completion of involved tasks and activities. Following these guidelines will be useful as you develop user-friendly instructions:

- Use a step-by-step format for tasks requiring more than a few steps. Using a step-by-step format helps the reader separate each step more clearly and see the progression of actions.
- Include graphic depictions as necessary and relevant to illustrate and simplify steps.
- Include safety tips as needed. Place the tip with the relevant step if the tip pertains to that step. Place any safety tip associated with the entire operation before the first step.

Example:

I use this example as I teach instructions; most business students have experience with Excel by the time they take my classes; however, very few have used it to perform regression analysis. We discuss the need and uses for a manual for that task and then consider what should go in it. An example of such a manual is shown in the following section. (Note that the screen shot figures are not actually included here, though their placement is indicated.)

Sample Manual (Excerpt)

Using Excel for Regression Analysis

These instructions provide information to help the reader understand how to perform regression analysis using Excel. The instructions are designed for users with some experience with Excel, particularly in creating a table and performing basic math functions such as summing and averaging.

Overview

Regression analysis is a statistical operation in which one studies data and their relationship to each other toward understanding how independent variables influence a dependent variable. The analysis results in the development of a line graph or equation like $y = mx - nz + b$; in which x and z are different independent variables, and y is the dependent variable. m and n represent coefficients for each independent variable.

Regression analysis can help understand quantitative relationships between variables involved in an outcome—sales forecasting, for example, or operations management. Regression analysis can also help understand the impact a given variable has on the outcome; for example, how much rainfall in a particular period affects demand for umbrellas in that period; or how much price level affects sales of umbrellas.

Dos and Don'ts

Regression analysis can be used for forecasting estimation and understanding quantitative relationships as described above. However, it should not be used as a sole tool for either of those. The output of regression analysis is a "best fit" line that may include substantial variance, which would be reported. The variance suggests how reliable the equation may be as a forecasting tool.

Avoid using insufficient data within regression analysis; it relies on ANOVA principles, and is sensitive to the amount of data included. Using a small amount of data points may result in more variance, making the line less reliable as a tool for analysis.

Instructions

1. Create and save a table of the data you wish to analyze. This is the most labor intensive step, and any data not saved may be lost if the computer crashes. Figure 8.1 shows a sample table.

Figure 8.1 Sample table

Figure 8.2 Dialog box for Data Analysis—Regression

2. Open dialog box for data, and click on "data analysis." See Figure 8.2.
3. ….[Instructions would also include information about how to read the output such as the coefficients, R value and other statistical values included.]

Trouble Shooting

[Use this section to address various common problems the user might encounter. For each identified problem, provide the following information.]

1. Identify the problem or symptoms (e.g., wrong column is reported as dependent variable).
2. Explain why the error occurred. (e.g., wrong column was entered as dependent variable; wrong column for at least one independent variable may also be involved, consequently; or, two columns were inputted as dependent variables).
3. Indicate how to correct it (e.g., input correct column).

Discussion

Note that the audience in the example is clearly identified in the manual's introduction. This element is important, because the first step is to create a table. A user with no background with Excel will not be able to complete that step. That user would require a different manual.

Even though the user has experience with Excel, he or she may not know what regression analysis is or how to use it. That information is also included. There are several steps involved with regression analysis; so the step-by-step format is ideal, including screen shots with each step to reinforce what the action should look like on the screen. Screen shots can allay fears users have by providing an image of what their screens will look like.

Applying the Formula to the Development of Manuals

The *situation* connected to any manual is that a new procedure needs to be learned by someone who may or may not have any familiarity with the task. The *desired action or response* is that they learn the new task and be able to perform it effectively. As indicated above, integrating graphics will address some of the *audience's needs*.

Instructions that include many graphics—especially diagrams of the process—are valuable for complex and lengthy processes. Consider how most people "read" instructions; most people will glance at instructions, depending on the complexity of the task. If a diagram is provided, they will focus attention on it. If the graphic shows a process, they are able to review that diagram and understand the process better and more efficiently than if they only read steps associated with the task. So the principle of visual dominance is evident; include as many graphics as possible; this may contribute, in fact, to the minimalist manual.

Applying other attributes of the formula relative to audience considerations, though, can include rewards, mirroring, and addressing any fears:

Rewards:

> What will motivate this person to respond a certain way (What reward can I offer?)?
> Perhaps the person will value being able to do a greater variety of tasks, contributing to their value to the company, with potential for promotion or a salary raise.

> How can I phrase the message so that reward is explicitly stated?

Mirroring:

> What does the audience think of me?

> What of my attributes or qualities does the audience value or admire?
> Perhaps the audience values my position in enabling their value to be recognized.

> How can I appeal to that perception?
> What attributes or qualities of my audience do I value or admire?
> Perhaps I value their ability to learn task quickly.

> How can I integrate those into my message?
> What terms can I use that my audience values and will get their attention?
> "Promotion," "Value to the company," "Raise."

Fears:

> What about this situation may invoke fear in my audience?

Any new endeavor can bring about some degree of fear.

Do I want to raise fear to provide some kind of motivation toward action?

Expressing how learning the task may increase the person's value to the company may motivate them to want to learn the task out of fear they may be perceived as less valuable if they do not learn it—an appeal to reward neurons.

How can I defuse or minimize that fear for my audience?

To what from their experiences might my audience compare this situation, and how can I help them overcome that fear or the fear they experienced before?

Describe how the task is similar to something they already know about, or that it is easy to learn.

Mode of Delivery:

How can I best deliver this message to get the desired response from my audience?

Again, a combination of manual (writing that includes several graphics or a clear comprehensive diagram) and hands-on learning is best to facilitate efficient learning.

Case 8.1 provides application of the principles related to development of manuals.

Case 8.1 Managing a Task through Instructions

Situation

Develop a short manual for one of the tasks associated with a recent job you had or one you currently have.

Tasks

1. Include the following sections in your instruction manual: an overview of the task; when it would be performed (Special situations? Normal part of job?), performance instructions

(step-by-step), including any graphics and safety tips; and a trouble-shooting section.

2. Consider the questions related to audience and how to motivate the audience to want to learn about the task (beyond continued employment). How can you engage mirror neurons with graphics?

3. Place each graphic with the step associated with it; or provide a single, comprehensive graphic—that clearly shows the process—that the reader can refer to as they read the text.

4. Reflect on your set of instructions; how would you explain to someone else your links between the product (instructions) and responses to the audience consideration questions? Write your reflection using up to 100 words.

CHAPTER 9

Oral Presentations and In-Person Meetings

Attending a presentation and being in the same room with the speaker brings about a very different communication experience than reading her words. A physical proximity between speaker and audience creates a different rhetorical effect. In this chapter, we consider how nonverbal attributes of the message further affect the rhetoric of the message, which can affect a decision regarding mode of delivery. It may be most convenient to send an e-mail to a coworker, but the message may be more effective for a few reasons if you meet with them in person.

Social Presence

The concept of "*Social Presence Theory*" posits that the more one is perceived as "real," the closer another feels to that person. Consider a comparison between online classes and face-to-face classes; or consider the experience of an in-person meeting versus a series of related exchanges that occur via e-mail with others whom you have never met in person. If you have ever taken an online class, how "close" did you feel to the other students or the teacher? Unless you had met them before in another class or setting, you likely did not feel very "close" to them. If you have taken face-to-face courses, you experience the other students and the instructor physically. You see them; you can touch them (shake their hand); you can talk to them and hear their voice. You feel much "closer" to them, and that exchange is very different.

As a class reflection activity, my team and I once had our students respond to the question of whether the required group assignment should be changed to an individual assignment. The classroom students almost unanimously indicated a preference for it to remain as a group assignment, whereas the web-based students were mixed. Most web-based students felt it should stay a group assignment, but they admitted it was difficult because of the online setting. Obviously, there is the challenge of coordinating schedules to meet (technically, web-based students do not *have* to meet face-to-face or in any real time setting; they are not required to do anything outside of the electronic environment). There is also often a lack of trust in group members, because they do not know whether particular group members are actually doing the work until they post it for review. In some cases with a group member who procrastinates too long, it may be too late, and the others take up that person's work. As such, the notion of social presence is the highest it can be when the communication occurs between people in face-to-face contact with someone in the same room.

Dress

In addition to physical proximity's effect on closeness and trust, dress can also enhance the effect of an in-person encounter. As I mentioned in *The Neuroscience of Multimodal Persuasive Messages*,[1] studies find that people are attracted to others who are similar to them. Political advertisers understand this and try to integrate particular dress in certain messages. If the politician is speaking about education policy, he may dress as teachers might dress. If the appeal is directed at the general public, his dress may be less formal. If the message pertains to business policy, he will dress as a business professional.

Sometimes, though, the audience may be persuaded more by someone who portrays some expertise they lack but recognize as being of value to them. A popular example of this is the person wearing a doctor's lab coat tells the general public that smoking is bad for their health. The message is considered more authoritative than if that person dressed casually—looking like a member of the general public—made the same statement. The person dressed as a doctor is a member of a community that has expertise in healthy lifestyles, while the other speaker is not. If the doctor was not dressed as a doctor, she would need to acknowledge explicitly her professional status in order for the message to have the same effect. The image of the doctor wearing the lab coat makes the statement for her, giving their message some degree of credibility. A manager or executive may dress more nicely than her employees dress, even as all are dressed professionally; because she exhibits a different position than they do, requiring a higher standard or expectation.

Much of the rhetoric related to dress is derived from the dynamics of neural plasticity—how neurons develop and react to certain stimuli over time. It is through conversations and experience that people learn how to react to stimuli, including one's dress. For example, one who was born in the last few decades cannot understand why everyone in a television show from the 1960s is wearing a suit or dress outside of work. The viewer is used to wearing casual clothing outside of word and is accustomed to seeing few people in public wearing formal dress, except as an expectation of their jobs or for a formal occasion.

While you may understand that it is natural to wear a business suit in a workplace environment, you may feel awkward wearing a suit at all. I am aware of a few business students who went to business job interviews wearing a polo shirt and khaki pants. It was not that they did not have a suit; it was just that they thought it acceptable to wear "dressy-casual" to an interview. In each case, they were turned away without the interview actually occurring. Their perception of what was acceptable fell below the employer's expectations of acceptable professional dress for the interview, resulting in a negative outcome for the applicant.

Imagine a conference room environment, with fifteen people at a meeting that is scheduled to last two hours. There may be a couple of people who become disruptive, talking to each other and giggling while the person conducting the meeting is speaking. Others in the room notice the behavior and are distracted by it. The disruptive pair responds differently to approaches to quiet them. At first, the person conducting the meeting gives them a look to quiet them down; they quiet down for a few minutes, but the disruption occurs again several minutes later. The leader asks them to quiet down, and they do so. This pattern happens once more during the meeting.

The leader's clothing may impact perceived authority. Managers and executives tend to wear nice business suits. Dress could reinforce the manager's position of authority as well as model professionalism. Nevertheless, the disruptive pair continues their behavior, and others at the meeting seem to understand the manager's effort to quiet the pair. The disruptive pair does not respond favorably to the manager's message, dress, or position. Perhaps, they value each other's behavior or attitude and mirror each other's behavior to reinforce their membership in the group. Nevertheless, the manager and others in the room observe a problem.

With about 45 minutes left in the meeting, the pair becomes loud again. Another person attending the meeting, male or female, gets up, walks over to the pair and says assertively, "I'm trying to listen and contribute. Please be quiet." The pair reacts to the message immediately and is quiet the rest of the meeting. The message attained its desired response. How?

While the pair may be responding positively to the other person's verbal statement, neural dynamics related to their position as a peer as well as dress may be at work in this example. The statement itself focuses on the speaker's perspective relative to an effort to be a good employee and help the company—a reasonable goal of the meeting. It, further, may represent the values of others in the meeting. That the person who confronted the pair is a peer places him or her in a different position than that of the manager. However, the way the person is dressed could affect the pair's response, too. The one who confronted the group may wear an outfit typical of the others. The person may even dress more nicely than the normal wear most of the others usually wear. Either of these elicits mirror neurons, reinforcing that the person is a peer. However, if the person dressed more nicely than how one may typically dress, it may affect the mirror dynamics as well as other neural dynamics.

What if the person was wearing very nice business attire, almost on par with the manager's or executive's suit? The person may appear more professional. The disruptive pair may respond to the business attire, because that person looks more professional. The person is dressed differently than the rest of the group, but in a positive way relative to the setting.

While the manager was trying to discourage the disruptive behavior in a subtle way, the one who confronted the pair walked to their place and told them, rather than asked them, to be quiet. The pair may have been afraid to challenge that person because of the fear of perceived aggression. As such, dynamics related to the amygdala and hippocampus are involved. It created an element of fear in the audience.

Again, the amygdala is concerned with survival. Further, the hippocampus helps recall memories so that we understand how we reacted to a given situation in the past; however, if that situation was a negative experience, perhaps related to an act of aggressive against us, we recall that negativity. We make a decision on how to respond based on recollections of those memories.

Consider how the way one is dressed can influence how the audience responds to a message. Much like the messages discussed in Chapter 5, the nonverbal attributes enhance the verbal message to generate a different reaction from the audience than just the verbal message may have. If the student had sent the message to the students in an e-mail after class, it could not have had the same visual effects.

Proximity

Prior experience is part of the neural dynamics, but these all were influenced because the action occurred with the participants in the same physical location. The example shows how the mode of delivery can affect the impact of the message. The encounter described above occurred with considerable physical proximity. E-mail and video conferencing tools enable one to communicate without fear of a physical encounter; a reader cannot be physically harmed if verbally attacked through e-mail. Further, while the speaker's dress may be visible in a video-conference, the lack of physical presence with the audience lessens its potential effect. However, the message has a different impact when the speaker is face-to-face with the audience.

I alluded to the concept of social presence before and how technology can create the perception of close physical proximity between communicants. The more visual and real-time interaction the technology can facilitate, the higher the level of social presence. Face-to-face is considered the highest level of social presence; so, if the speaker and audience are in the same physical location at the time the message is presented, it is the highest level of social presence. Generally, studies find that there is a greater response to persuasive messages within higher social presence contexts; so, it is relevant to include it among the dynamics affecting persuasion. In a situation in which one wants to persuade a single person or small group, it is likely most effective to do it in-person. That is, an in-person meeting may facilitate leaner communication than an e-mail would, since the nonverbal elements—tone, dress, facial expression, and others, such as scent and touch—enhance the verbal elements. This combination of verbal and nonverbal elements facilitate efficiencies relative to conciseness, clarity and impact.

Obviously, an oral presentation that accompanies a written proposal allows for more exchange between the speaker(s) and the audience. However, physical attributes of the speaker can influence audience reception. As I wrote in *The Neuroscience of Persuasive Messages* (2017), "A presentation from an attractive person may be received better than one delivered by an unattractive person. A presentation delivered from an attractive person wearing a nice-smelling fragrance—perfume or cologne—may be better received than one from someone who is not wearing cologne or perfume."[2]

It is reported that, "Nike discovered that they could increase the intent to purchase by 80 percent through the introduction of scent into their stores. Another survey at a petrol station with a mini-mart reported that the aroma of coffee helped boost sales of the beverage by a whopping 300 percent" (paragraph 7).[3] According to another study by the Smell & Taste Research Foundation, "[m]any of the subjects in the study reported that they were willing to pay $10 more for Nike sneakers placed in scented rooms, than those placed in an unscented one"[4] Floral scents appeal to the hippocampus—pleasant memories and images in our mind. While the scent activates the hippocampus, mirror neurons or reward neurons are activated by the presenter's image or position.

Generally, the handshake has emerged as a part of the professional greeting between professionals who do not interact frequently. In addition to the stated "Hello," the communicants exchange a pleasant handshake and eye contact. Neither of those—handshake or eye contact—occurs with an e-mail, letter, or report. Several websites offer tips to enhance the impact these have in an exchange; nevertheless, neural phenomena help to explain that effect.

Another example of the effect physical proximity and what you do with it can have is the experience of a colleague who proposed to a major technology company to provide a grant for computer classrooms that included additional instructional technologies. The company manufactures and sells computers—mostly hardware. My colleague brought one of the company's laptop computers that she borrowed from another colleague to facilitate her presentation to the technology company managers, consciously aware of the effect doing so could have.

My colleague is a devout user of computers produced by one of the company's competitors. Using one of the company's machines placed her in a more favorable light than if she had used the competitor's machine during the presentation. She was able to persuade the company to provide the grant for the computer or technology classrooms.

Graphics, Slide Design, and Oral Presentations

Graphics tend to be used extensively in oral presentations. While a graphic can be formatted the same way for a print document and for a presentation slide, it may need to be modified on the slide. Slide design involves formatting information on the slide so that it is visible by all in the audience. However, just as with a graphic in a document, be sure to enlarge the graphic so all can view it clearly. Further, avoid placing a lot of text on a single slide; viewers do not want to have to read a portion of your presentation script. So limit the amount of information on a slide.

You can use colors to enhance the image and make the presentation more dynamic. Select colors that include enough contrast so they appear clearly for the audience; make sure there is enough contrast between the background and any text or graphic so the text or graphic stands out. Sometimes when trying to integrate several colors, a presenter winds up placing yellow text on an orange background; the text is not visible. The theme and mood of the presentation will also help you decide on color selections, as particular colors are associated with certain subjects and attitudes.

A presenter must also be concerned with the use of space in slide design. Though Prezi is growing in popularity, we will focus on PowerPoint as the primary slide show tool. PowerPoint continues to be prominent in business settings for two main reasons: (1) more people are comfortable with it because of wide accessibility and prior experience with it), and (2) it was designed with business presentations in mind.

Some graphic experts, including Edward Tufte and David Walbert, have given PowerPoint low marks as a presentation aid, citing its simplicity.[5, 6, 7] However, in business settings, this simplicity can be a strength. The templates provided for slide development facilitate short bursts of information using bulleted points, and specific information can be easily emphasized with color highlighting and larger and different fonts. Its tools also allow for "animation" within a slide to help focus the audience's attention by revealing or emphasizing text when the presenter is ready to talk about it.

Walbert developed a rubric for assessing slide show effectiveness.[8] Among the specific criteria for assessing content, which are often applied in assessing traditional forms of writing, he identified focus, organization, development, and mechanics. Focus pertains to how well the product addresses a specific issue or topic. Organization pertains to how logically the presentation flows from one point to the next. Development pertains to examples and use of outside sources to illustrate and clarify a give point. Finally, the print-linguistic text on each slide ought to reflect proficiency with conventions of spelling, grammar, and punctuation.

Linking Walbert's guidelines to the neuroscience formula, we can consider focus to be how well each slide addresses some portion of that purpose. This helps to eliminate irrelevant material; something Tufte also encourages. Including only the most relevant information helps the audience to focus on the particular point of the slide or set of slides.

Content and development could include the elements of audience considerations, since responses to those questions guide development of the content. These would be focused on meeting the information needs of the audience while affecting neural response.

Organization simply applies principles of good writing or communication generally; the slide show should flow smoothly from one point to another point. In creating an effect, for example, a proposal should move from identifying the problem and helping the audience understand why it is a problem that needs to be addressed, to identifying a solution or possible solutions, and their strengths or weaknesses in addressing the problem, to identifying and explaining which is recommended and how to implement it. Depending on time limitations, one could eliminate the discussion of different options and go directly from the identification of the problem and why it needs to be addressed to identifying the recommendations and its justification.

Too often, students will orally repeat text on a slide, as if using the slide as a script. This is not productive. As a visual aid, PPT should supplement or complement the narration. This advice differs from what is practiced in many instructional settings, where a slide for a lecture may facilitate note taking.

Slide design involves use of space on the slide and size of text or images as well as color. There should be enough contrast between the text and background that the text stands out. Any text or images should be large enough that those in the back of the room can view the information on the slide easily. Avoid putting too much text on a single slide—often a problem when using a slide show as a script.

The oral delivery should be complemented by the visual elements. By facilitating use of both the audial and visual channels, people can better process information than they can when too much of one system is used.[9] Case 9.1 provides the opportunity to apply the principles of graphic design to the creation of presentation slides.

Case 9.1 Page Design Versus Slide Design

Situation:

Refer to the information in Chapter 4 about the market study I prepared for the regional campus. That study reported findings pertaining to addressing an enrollment decline; the particular information shown pertained to the current enrollments in various major programs.

Task

Develop TWO slides that would be part of a slide show in which you report on the market study. Consider the amount of information you should integrate into each slide, color contrasts, and audience considerations.

Case 9.2 allows you to apply what you have learned about message strategy in oral delivery.

Case 9.2 Verbal and Nonverbal
Attributes of the Message

Situation

Consider an upcoming meeting or class presentation in which you will participate.

Tasks

1. Use the audience consideration questions that follow to develop an outline of what you plan to say and how you plan to say it.

   Rewards:
   What will motivate this person to respond a certain way (What reward can I offer?)?
   How can I phrase the message so that reward is explicitly stated?

   Mirroring:
   What does the audience think of me?
   What of my attributes or qualities does the audience value or admire?
   How can I appeal to that perception?
   What attributes or qualities of my audience do I value or admire?
   How can I integrate those into my message?
   What terms can I use that my audience values and will get their attention?

   Fears:
   What about this situation may invoke fear in my audience?
   Do I want to raise fear to provide some kind of motivation toward action?
   How can I defuse or minimize that fear for my audience?
   To what from their experiences might my audience compare this situation, and how can I help them overcome that fear or the fear they experienced before?

Mode of Delivery:

Face-to-face, of course; but what visual attributes you can integrate or implement to optimize that delivery?

1. Compose the message script that you will use in your presentation.
2. What visual considerations will you try to apply (dress, posture, facial expressions, demeanor, or props)? Describe them and the effect you hope to accomplish with them in a short narrative.

CHAPTER 10

Wrapping It Up with Principles and Caveats

Each interaction between humans involves understanding one's audience, specifically what motivates them and what affects their decisions to respond a certain way. This book has presented ways to think about how neural activity influences these responses. The several questions related to audience considerations that we have considered represent detailed analysis that can affect how an audience responds to a message. In this chapter we will summarize those points to create a more concise listing of the considerations and also consider some caveats related to these principles.

Considerations

In Chapter 1, we considered some primary neuroscientific concepts to consider relative to an audience. These included: mirror neurons, reward neurons, prior experience, and fear. The audience considerations may be viewed more simply by focusing on generalizations about the effect these concepts have on response. Table 10.1 repeats the information from Table 1.1 that appeared earlier in the book; however, I have added a few caveats.

In the simplest terms, put yourself in your audience's place; how would you want the message conveyed to motivate you toward action while recognizing your concerns about the particular situation?

Explicitly and Genuinely Mirror the Audience's Values

Understand what your audience values in their work and other people, including you. Culture plays a role in this; however, so, too, does upbringing. Get to know your audience. However, avoid "pretending"

Table 10.1 NeuroCommunicative model with caveats

Rewards:	Mirroring:
What will motivate this person to respond a certain way (What reward can I offer?)? How can I phrase the message so that reward is explicitly stated? CAVEAT: *Theory X (unmotivated employee) or Theory Y (motivated employee) Spectrum: May need to customize to the person.*	What does the audience think of me (including my trustworthiness)? What of my attributes or qualities does the audience value or admire? How can I appeal to that perception? What attributes or qualities of my audience do I value/admire? How can I integrate those into my message? What terms can I use that my audience values and will get their attention? CAVEAT: *Model desired behaviors. Don't mirror undesirable communication behaviors.*
Fears:	Mode of Delivery:

What about this situation may invoke fear in my audience?
 	
Do I want to raise fear to provide some kind of motivation toward action?
 	
How can I defuse or minimize that fear for my audience?
 	
To what from their experiences might my audience compare this situation, and how can I help them overcome that fear or the fear they experienced before?
 	
CAVEAT: *Understand Good use or Bad use*
	How can I best deliver this message to get the desired response from my audience?
	    Writing—letter or e-mail? [only print-linguistic text]
	    Phone call? [only aural]
	    In person? [multimodal]
	
	CAVEAT: *Available mode(s): Conference call may be more effective than e-mail or phone as a substitute for in-person.*

to value similar things that your audience values; Pillay (2011) notes that our neurons help us to understand when someone is not genuine.[1] Several studies also note this relative to trust.[2]

Understand as well what your employees and supervisors value in terms of the persona and character of a leader or executive, and mirror that. Model desired professional behaviors. Indeed, others tend to look to the leader or manager to understand exceptional skills and behaviors that they should mirror.

Be Explicit with Rewards

Again, understand what your audience perceives as rewards (and penalties) associated with their work and what actions you want to get from them.

Talk about how they may directly benefit, as well as how the organization benefits or is rewarded if they do something. Develop fair rewards, too; people understand fairness and respond negatively to seeing unfairness around them. It affects trust.

Consider applying positive language when describing negative items—such as weak performance. Offering some kind of hope of a reward for improved performance can help the audience accept changes more readily than mere threats of being fired.

Use Stories

Narratives are a way of offering details about successful implementation of projects and a way of offering hope of successful change. Everyone fears change because of uncertainties. The more people understand that change can lead to rewards for everyone, the easier it is for them to accept change.

Recognize Good Use and Bad Use of Fear

Fear is associated with any kind of change. However, we need to moderate fear carefully. Some fear is good to have, because the will to live or survive is powerful. We will do what we think we need to do to survive. The easier we perceive that action to be, the more hopeful the situation becomes. When too much fear arises, a situation may seem hopeless. Whether an audience expresses fear, understand there may be some fear implicitly integrated into a situation.

Express the potential fear and how the audience can overcome it. While acknowledging potential drawbacks if it fails, nursing the fear, convey rewards employees will receive (organization-wide or even individual employee-specific rewards) if the change is successful. Convey contingency plans if there is risk.

Caveats

Various dynamics affect an audience's response to a message and will, therefore, impact your message strategy.

Office Politics?

Office politics should be considered within the various portions of the set of questions related to audience. For example, if you understand that a manager may "pull rank," consider why he might do it. Is it because he has seen others use it and it worked for them? That is a consideration of mirror neurons and prior experience that may also link to reward neurons if those others were somehow rewarded for their behavior. If he knows that you have little recourse for his behavior, he may be doing it merely because someone once did it to him; that would be related to prior experience.

I encourage you to learn what you can about your employees through informal discussions or dialogue to help them recognize their prior experiences and motivations. Some opportunities can emerge from the job interview; others can come from lunch meetings and light conversation. Such conversations engage a personal bonding of sorts that helps the other person feel less afraid of leadership. Consequently, such encounters have an effect on amygdala-related dynamics. So, while you are helping employees overcome a fear, you can also learn more about them toward understanding how to communicate future messages.

"Going Over the Boss's Head"

Sometimes an individual needs to "go over the manager's head." This is a difficult situation that quickly becomes awkward because of lasting effects. Once you have gone over your boss' head, your boss may not trust you to come to her directly. I have encountered such situations, though I do not present any as examples here because of the awkwardness. However, I provide some tips to manage such situations if you find yourself in such a situation—having to go over your supervisor's head to get desired results.

In situations requiring upper-management's involvement, approach the supervisor first and ascertain her response. Be sure to help her understand *WHY* she needs to act on your concern or make upper management aware of it, applying audience consideration principles. This transaction may be connected to mirror neurons (your supervisor wanting to be like upper management) or reward neurons (potential reward/bonus for bringing it to upper management's awareness).

A way around the awkwardness may be to offer the message in a conversation with the higher level manager you are trying to reach with your idea or issue. If the topic comes up in conversation and you offer a suggestion in that setting, it seems less like you have "gone over the boss's head." If you have talked to your boss about it, you can even mention that:

> I told Susan about this, but I don't know if she has done anything with it yet. She may be thinking of different ways to address it....

Such a statement makes your boss look diligent. It also allows the boss's boss to bring up the issue without it looking like a political mess. In fact, it may come across as an invitation to talk it over with that boss:

> Steve mentioned..., and it sounds like it could be a problem. He said he talked to you about it. What ideas have you come up with?

The awkwardness of going over the boss's head can be minimized. If set up skillfully, the exchange can be productive for all.

Clarity, Conciseness, and Narrative

You may have noticed that the examples I used in the latter chapters seemed relatively lengthy in terms of business style. As I indicated previously, these are messages that are, in many cases, difficult. Effective communication (not just clarity for the audience, but the audience's acceptance of the action one is communicating or getting the desired response from the audience) requires some narrative elements to elicit favorable neural response. Narratives appeal to several neural elements, and they can help get the desired response. These narrative elements contribute to a longer message; though, one should not consider the narrative elements to be "fluff." As I wrote in an earlier chapter, each part of the message is doing something toward facilitating a desired response.

Understand your audience's needs relative to "stories" that may help them understand and accept a given action being implemented. Very little narrative may be needed; or a lot may be needed. If you know of a change that occurred somewhere else and that proved to be successful not just in terms of profit but also in terms of ease of transition, share that story. Employees at all levels are concerned about a company's financial results, but they are also concerned about how a change affects them. That effect is not just in terms of employment; it is also relative to the stress of changing a usual habit.

The Value of Failure Stories

No one likes to, or wants to, fail. In several chapters I've echoed the value of narratives and encouraged the telling of success stories to help the audience understand that a change can work out well. However, there is value in failure narratives, if they are presented carefully. These are stories about an initiative or project that you tried to implement and that failed. Such stories help to lend credibility to your position while helping an audience understand that you are human. Change involves risks; risk-taking is part of leadership.

While talking about failures, talk about what you learned from them. Talk about how something that failed lead to a success, even if it helped to identify a limitation that could not be changed. How did you address that limitation, or a similar one, with the next project? Some years ago, we tried to coordinate a team assignment across multiple sections of a single course, and it did not go well. Teams of four students each were created from six sections; yet in some cases only one person from a team may have been in a given section while in another team, two or three members were in the same section. The more diverse the group was in terms of the number of different sections of the course involved in the group, the more challenging students found it to collaborate. It was also difficult to coordinate assessment of the submissions, because the teaching team had to be trained toward a normed assessment; that is, everyone had to understand how to grade so grading from one instructor to another would be consistent. No single grader would be deemed "easier" or "harder" than another.

I had applied multisection teams previously with success, but those were set up with pairs of students from each section involved in four-person groupings. No one felt "alone" as they worked in class on the assignment. Recognizing the challenges related to the larger multisection assignment on both ends—students and instructors—we dropped the assignment for future semesters. However, the new policy was that instructors were allowed to arrange multisection team assignments limited to two of their own sections or closely coordinated with one other instructor's section to assure ease of coordination for both students and instructors.

Considering length of a narrative, the story I just conveyed takes less than 1½ minutes to share orally.

The Dismissal or Layoff Message

I intentionally omitted what most would consider to be the most challenging message to deliver; the one in which you acknowledge to someone that they are being let go. One hopes not to have to convey such a message; however, the nature of a leadership position means it will likely occur at some point. I have never been in the position, but I write based on exchanges with others and their experiences.

The message depends heavily on the nature of the reason for letting the person go. For example, if one is being let go in a cost-cutting effort but has been a good employee, that message will differ from the one involving a weak employee.

- Cost-Cutting a Good Employee. While buffering the message with recognition of the person's hard work (mirror/reward), acknowledge what criterion influenced the decision, so the person understands it is not a personal issue you had with his work. Also, if possible, convey hope that he can be rehired at some point if available. The more hopeful the message is, the better.

    Also, if possible, create a transition program for such employees, helping them prepare for the job search and providing ways to facilitate finding other employment. A layoff will invoke the amygdala quite a bit—survival is challenged and jeopardized. Just as with any kind of fear, the more explicit the appearance of an effort to help address the fear the more the person feels he can trust you and the company, and he leaves feeling better than if no support was offered.

- Dismissing a Bad Employee. There are employees at any level who do not seem to care much about their work and take each day of work as a burden. They recognize that they need a paycheck to pay for their lifestyle—whatever that lifestyle may involve—but they are not enthusiastic about work. This demeanor can affect the quality of their work negatively, putting them in the position of being a liability to the organization.

    Principles of good leadership generally encourage working with such a person to help her improve, but it does not always work well. In such cases, it is possible to offer a short message, having warned her previously about consequences and reminding her of those acknowledgments. Remind her of the situation, your efforts to help address it, her lack of improvement, and the need for you now to act on the consequences that were previously discussed.

    The dismissed employee may still blame you for the dismissal, but others in the organization will understand the fairness of your actions.

What About "Me?"

In the first chapter of this book, we considered the attributes of the messenger that are included inherently in the various elements of the message. Further, we considered that it may at times be important to omit some information from the message that the messenger may be aware of because it could negatively affect the desired response. Consider the following caveats relevant to those situations.

Discuss your concerns about a situation and potential message with others at your level in the organization or higher to ascertain how credible your concerns are; this may change your perception of the situation and your understanding of how others perceive it. These conversations may also help you to understand what information is relevant to a message and what is not.

A manager may fear telling an employee about pressures the manager faces because they seem irrelevant to the employee. In many cases, I do not hesitate to acknowledge pressures I face from others, because it is important for my audience to understand what is motivating a given action or message. Such information may help me gain the desired response; my audience will take appropriate action because they understand I am not the only one who has something to gain or lose based on the actions.

However, I do omit some information if I perceive it will negatively affect the response. If a certain detail could incite panic or express likelihood that a task will fail, the audience may quit the effort associated with completing the task. "Why should I even try if the effort is for nothing?" A sports coach may perceive that the game is lost, but he still needs to get the best effort out of the players. So he may omit from a pep talk his concerns about how a loss will affect his own job or how a few players seem to not be trying hard anymore. The coach is aware of these issues, but conveying them won't help the team play well. Likewise, a manager needs to continue to motivate her employees even when a situation seems hopeless. In Chapter 2, we considered the impact of positive and negative language. Omitting certain details may help the message seem more positive than if the details were included. The audience may, consequently, respond more favorably to the message.

Consider the recommendation letter scenarios presented in Chapter 2. In one of the sample responses, all the details were included; in a few, they were not included. I posed the question about which was most effective and which was least effective. How did the inclusion of details, or lack thereof, affect the audience's response?

Science Versus Art

I mentioned a caveat in the first chapter of this book, and I end the book reminding the reader of it; communication is an art form. One person may react a certain way to a given message, while a second person reacts very differently to the same message. The tips and discussion in this book attempt to offer insights into ways to improve communication effectiveness by providing insight as to how messages affect neural dynamics and what is involved in shaping those dynamics.

So many factors influence development of neurons and those neural dynamics associated with responding to a message that it is very difficult to predict that a given message will work for a particular audience. Through study and practice of recommended communication strategies, you can achieve greater success in getting your point across effectively.

Glossary

Amygdala: Part of limbic system, located at the end of the hippocampus. It is a set of neurons associated with basic responses and emotions such as fear and pleasure, particularly fear.

Analysis: Systematic approach to reviewing data collected through research or from observations toward identifying findings or conclusions about that data.

Anecdotal Information: A single example or experience used to illustrate something; for example, describing how a company uses a particular resource.

Claim Message: In business correspondence, it refers to a message requesting an adjustment for defective goods or services. A customer or client recognizes a defect in the product or service and approaches the company to address the problem.

Colavita Visual Dominance Effect: Term to describe the phenomenon that visual stimuli are acquired or noticed faster than any other stimulus. Consequently, the brain perceives visual information before it perceives any other kind of stimulus, giving visual stimuli a position of dominance over other kinds of stimuli.

Cost-Benefit Analysis: Process of considering the costs of implementing a project or program and the benefits the program may bring. Generally, if the benefits outweigh the costs, the program is perceived positively.

Economic Analysis: Systematic approach to reviewing economic data toward ascertaining conclusions about the economic conditions or financial aspects of implementing a project.

Experiential Learning: Learning through real performance of a task. Often linked to internship experiences or through substantive case study activities.

Feasibility Analysis: Systematic approach to ascertaining whether a proposed program or project is possible or feasible. Feasibility may be considered relative to any number of criteria, including but not limited to: economic analysis, technological availability, and organizational mission.

Hippocampus: Portion of brain associated with memory, facilitated through experiences. It is part of the limbic system of the brain, closely linked to memory, emotion, and learning.

Mirror Neurons: Type of brain neurons that helps one to learn new tasks through mimicking others as they perform that task; also associated with the development of empathy.

Multimodal Neurons: Neurons that are able to process information from multiple modes of representation—for example, auditory, touch, visual. Some are bi-modal, processing stimuli from two modes of representation; while others may be tri-modal, processing stimuli from three different modes of representation.

Neural Plasticity: Term used to describe neurons that develop electrical bridges over time. As a given piece of information is learned through repetition, more links between neurons are formed, facilitating faster processing of that information. Conversely, if a task is not performed or information not used over a period of time, the individual may lose related connections, causing lack of remembrance of how to do the task or recall the information.

Prefrontal Cortex: Located near the front and among the last portions of the brain to develop, it is associated with decision making and complex problem solving. It is also associated with self-control, attention, and prioritizing of information.

Primary Research (also, Empirical Research): Systematic observation, experiment, or survey conducted by the researcher. It may be reported in a published work or used internally.

Secondary Research: Research findings or other information reported in published articles or books, or made available to an audience using other delivery methods.

Social Presence Theory: The degree to which communicators are perceived as being real or in each other's presence during communication; often linked to certain kinds of technology-mediated communication acts. Video conferencing tools such as Skype may facilitate high social presence (high level of perceived real presence) while e-mail facilitates low social presence.

SWOT [Strengths, Weaknesses, Opportunities, Threats] Analysis: Acronym representing the various aspects associated with a systematic approach to comparing a business's products and services to those of its competitors toward ascertaining competitive advantage. S and W represent an internal consideration of which products or services the company are doing well in the market (strengths) and which are not doing well (weaknesses). O and T represent external consideration of products or services offered by the company's competitors. Which competitor products or services are not doing well in the market (opportunities) and which are doing well (threats)? Products or services the company offers that are doing well and are positioned positively against competitors' products or services represent a competitive advantage for the company. Companies emphasize any competitive advantage in their marketing communications.

Uni-Modal Neurons: Neurons that are able to process information from only one mode of representation—for example, auditory, touch, visual.

Notes

Chapter 1

1. Morgan (2015).
2. Drucker (1989).
3. Aristotle (1991).
4. Cialdini (2013, pp. 25–42).
5. Conger (2013, pp. 67–89).
6. Hamm (2013, pp. 145–63).
7. Aristotle (1991).
8. Drucker (1989).
9. McGregor (1960).
10. Hutchins (1996).
11. Pinker (1997).
12. Azar (2010, pp. 36–38).
13. Pillay (2011).
14. Ramsay et al. (2013, pp. 1136–47).
15. Pillay (2011).
16. Perelman and Olbrechts-Tyteca (1969).
17. Moreno and Mayer (2000).
18. Bethge, Rotermund, and Pawelzik (2003, pp. 303–19).
19. Bremner and Spence (2008, pp. 335–36).
20. Colavita (1974, pp. 409–12).
21. Howard and Templeton (1966).
22. Welch and Warren (1986).
23. Colavita (1974, pp. 409–12).
24. Spence, Parise, and Chen (2012, pp. 529–56).
25. Pillay (2011).
26. Remley (2015).
27. Gee (2003).
28. Pinker (1997).
29. Mayer (2001).
30. Berlucchi and Buchtel (2009, pp. 307–19).
31. Zack (2017, pp. 86–90).

Chapter 2

1. Adams (2014).
2. Hansen and Hansen (2015).
3. Simonds (2013).
4. Simonds (2013).
5. Williams (1981, pp. 152–68).

Chapter 3

1. Dixon et al. (2017).

Chapter 4

1. Denning (2013).
2. Arnheim (1969).
3. Mitchell (1995).
4. Pinker (1997).
5. Arnheim (1969).
6. Mitchell (1995).
7. Arnheim (1969).
8. Hicks (1973).
9. Mitchell (1995).
10. Mayer (2001).

Chapter 5

1. Hamm (2013, pp. 145–163).
2. Remley (2017).

Chapter 6

1. Hamm (2013, pp. 145–163).

Chapter 7

1. Hamm (2013, pp. 145–163).

Chapter 8

1. Remley (2015).
2. Kajikawa et al. (2012, pp. 65–98).
3. Kayser et al. (2012, pp. 99–114).
4. Moreno and Mayer (2000).
5. Munhall and Vatikiotis-Bateson (2004, pp. 177–188).
6. Moreno and Mayer (2000).
7. Carroll et al. (1988, pp. 73–102).
8. Pinker (1997).
9. Kalyuga (2005, pp. 325–336).
10. Mayer (2001).
11. Gee (2003).

Chapter 9

1. Remley (2017).
2. Remley (2017).
3. Cartwright (2014).
4. Tufte (2003).
5. Tufte (2006).
6. Walbert (n.d.).
7. Walbert (n.d.).
8. Baddeley (1986).
9. Schnotz (2005, pp. 49–60).

Chapter 10

1. Pillay (2011).
2. Zack (2017, pp. 86–90).

References

Adams, S. 2014. "The 10 Skills Employers Most Want in 2015 Graduates. *Forbes*. Retrieved from http://forbes.com/sites/susanadams/2014/11/12/the-10-skills-employers-most-want-in-2015-graduates/

Arnheim, R. 1969. *Visual Thinking*. Berkeley: University of California Press.

Aristotle. 1991. *The Art Of Rhetoric* (H.C. Lawson-Tancred, Trans). London: Penguin.

Azar, B. 2010. "More Powerful Persuasion." *Monitor on Psychology 41*, pp. 36–38. Retrieved from www.scn.ucla.edu/pdf/Persuasion-Monitor-2010.pdf (accessed June 3, 2013).

Baddeley, A.D. 1986. *Working Memory*. Oxford: Oxford UP.

Berlucchi, G., and H.A. Buchtel. 2009. "Neuronal Plasticity: Historical Roots and Evolution of Meaning." *Experimental Brain Research 192*, no. 3, pp. 307–19. doi:10.1007/s00221-008-1611-6

Bethge, M., D. Rotermund, and K. Pawelzik. 2003. "Optimal Neural Rate Coding Leads to Multimodal Firing Rate Distributions." *Computational Neural Systems 14*, pp. 303–19.

Bremner, A.J., and C. Spence. 2008. "Unimodal Experience Constrains While Multisensory Experiences Enrich Cognitive Construction." *Behavioral and Brain Sciences 31*, pp. 335–36.

Carroll, J.M., P.L.S. Kerker, J.R. Ford, and S. Mazur. 1988. "The Minimal Manual." In *Effective Documentation: What We Have Learned from Research*, ed. E. Doheny-Farina, 73–102. Cambridge: MIT Press.

Cartwright, S. 2014, December 23. "How and Why Businesses Make Use of Scent Marketing to Boost Sales." *Website Designs*. Retrieved from https://website-designs.com/online-marketing/scent-marketing/scent-marketing-to-boost-sales/ (accessed December 23, 2014).

Cialdini, R.A. 2013. "Harnessing the Science of Persuasion." In *on communication. HBR's 10 Must Reads Series*, pp. 25–42. Boston: Harvard Business Review Press. Originally published in *Harvard Business Review*, September 2001.

Colavita, F.B. 1974. "Human Sensory Dominance." *Perception & Psychophysics, 16*, pp. 409–12.

Conger, J.A. 2013. "The Necessary Art of Persuasion." In *on Communication. HBR's 10 Must Reads Series*, pp. 67–89. Boston: Harvard Business Review Press. Originally published in *Harvard Business Review*, May 1998.

Denning, S. 2013. "Telling Tales." In *on Communication. HBR's 10 must reads series*, pp. 115–130. Boston: Harvard Business Review Press. Originally published in *Harvard Business Review*, May 2004.

Dixon, M., L. Ponomareff, S. Turner, and R. DeLisi. January-February, 2017. "Consumers Want Results—Not Sympathy." *Harvard Business Review*, pp. 112–17.

Drucker, P.E. 1989. *The New Realities: In Government, and Politics/In Economics and Business/In Society and World View*. New York: Harper & Row.

Gee, J.P. 2003. *What Video Games Have to Teach Us About Learning and literacy*. New York: Palgrave McMillan.

Hamm, J. 2013. "The Five Messages Leaders Must Manage." In *On communication: HBR's 10 must reads series*, pp. 145–163. Boston: Harvard Business Review Press. Originally published in *Harvard Business Review*, May 2006.

Hansen, R.S., and K. Hansen. 2015. "What Do Employers Really Want? Top Skills and Values Employers Seek from Job Seekers. *Quint Careers*. Retrieved from http://quintcareers.com/job-skills-values/

Hicks, W. 1973. *Words and Pictures: The Literature of Journalism*. New York: Arno Press.

Howard, I.P., and W.B. Templeton. 1966. *Human Spatial Orientation*. London: Wiley.

Hutchins, E. 1996. *Cognition in the Wild*. Cambridge: MIT Press.

Kajikawa, Y., A. Falchier, G. Musacchia, P. Lakatos, and C. Schroeder. 2012. "Audiovisual Integration in Nonhuman Primates: A Window Into the Anatomy and Physiology of Cognition. In *The Neural Bases of Multisensory Processes*, eds. M. Murray and M. Wallace (eds.), 65–98. Boca Raton: CRC Press.

Kalyuga, S. 2005. "Prior Knowledge Principle in Multimedia Learning." In *The Cambridge Handbook of Multimedia Learning*, ed. R.E. Mayer, 325–36. Cambridge: Cambridge UP.

Kayser, C., C.I. Petkov, R. Remedios, and N.K. Logothetis. 2012. "Multisensory Influences on Auditory Processing: Perspectives from fMRI and Electrophysiology." In *The Neural Bases of Multisensory Processes*, eds. M. Murray and M. Wallace, 99–114. Boca Raton: CRC Press.

Mayer, R.E. 2001. *Multi-Media Learning*. Cambridge: Cambridge University Press.

McGregor, D. 1960. *The Human Side of Enterprise*. New York: McGrawHill.

Mitchell, W.J.T. 1995. *Picture Theory*. Chicago: University of Chicago Press.

Moreno, R., and R.E. Mayer. 2000. "A Learner-Centered Approach to Multimedia Explanations: Deriving Instructional Design Principles from Cognitive Theory." *Interactive Multimedia Electronic Journal of Computer-Enhanced Learning 2*, no. 2, pp. 12–20.

Morgan, J. 2015. "Why All Managers Must be Leaders." *Forbes*. Retrieved from https://forbes.com/sites/jacobmorgan/2015/01/21/why-all-managers-must-be-leaders/#7cd79ef7fd3b

Munhall, K.G., and E. Vatikiotis-Bateson. 2004. Spatial and Temporal Constraints on Audiovisual Speech Perception." In *The Handbook of Multisensory Processes*, eds. G. Calvert, C. Spence, and B.E. Stein, 177–88. Cambridge: MIT Press.

Perelman, C., and L. Olbrechts-Tyteca. 1969. *The New Rhetoric: A Treatise on Argumentation*. (Wilkinson, J., & and Weaver, P., Trans.). Notre Dame: University of Notre Dame Press.

Pillay, S.S. 2011. *Your Brain And Business. The Neuroscience of Great Leaders*. Upper Saddle River: Pearson/Financial Press.

Pinker, S. 1997. *How the Mind Works*. New York: W.W. Norton and Sons.

Ramsay, I.S., M.C. Yzer, M. Luciana, K.D. Vohs, and A.W. MacDonald. 2013. "Affective and Executive Network Processing Associated with Persuasive Antidrug Messages." *Journal of Cognitive Neuroscience 25*, no. 7, pp. 1136–47. doi:10.1162/jocn_a_00391

Remley, D. 2017. *The Neuroscience of Multimodal Persuasive Messages: Persuading the Brain*. New York: Routledge.

Remley, D. 2015. *How the Brain Processes Multimodal Technical Instructions*. Amityville: Baywood.

Schnotz, W. 2005. "An Integrated Model of Text and Picture Comprehension." In *The Cambridge handbook of multimedia learning*, ed. R.E. Mayer, 49–60. Cambridge: Cambridge UP.

Simonds, L. April 19, 2013. "Good Writing Can Help You Succeed." *Time*. Retrieved from http://business.time.com/2013/04/19/good-writing-can-help-you-succeed/

Spence, C., C. Parise, and Y. Chen. 2012. "The Colavita Visual Dominance Effect." In *The Neural Bases of Multisensory Processes*, eds. M. Murray and M. Wallace, 529–556. Boca Raton: CRC Press.

Tufte, E. 2003. *The Cognitive Style of PowerPoint*. Cheshire, CT: Graphics Press.

Tufte, E. 2006. *Beautiful Evidence*. Cheshire, CT: Graphics Press.

Walbert, D. n.d. "Evaluating Multimedia Presentations." Learn NC. Retrieved from http://learnnc.org/lp/pages/647

Welch, R., and D. Warren. 1986. "Intersensory Interactions." In *Handbook of Perception and Human Performance: Vol I. Sensory Processes and Human Performance*, eds. K. Boff, L. Kauffman, and J. Thomas. New York: Wiley.

Williams, J.M. 1981. "The Phenomenology of Error." *College Composition and Communication 32*, pp. 152–68. Retrieved from http://english.illinois.edu/-people-/faculty/schaffner/Williams%20Error.pdf

Zack, P.J. January-February, 2017. "The Neuroscience of Trust." *Harvard Business Review*, pp. 86–90.

Index

OTHER TITLES IN OUR CORPORATE COMMUNICATION COLLECTION

Debbie DuFrene, Stephen F. Austin State University, Editor

- *Technical Marketing Communication: A Guide to Writing, Design, and Delivery* by Emil B. Towner and Heidi L. Everett
- *Communication for Consultants* by Rita R. Owens
- *Zen and the Art of Business Communication: A Step-by-Step Guide to Improving Your Business Writing Skills* by Susan L. Luck
- *The Essential Guide to Business Communication for Finance Professionals* by Jason L. Snyder and Lisa A.C. Frank
- *Planning and Organizing Business Reports: Written, Oral, and Research-Based* by Dorinda Clippinger
- *Producing Written and Oral Business Reports: Formatting, Illustrating, and Presenting* by Dorinda Clippinger
- *How to Write Brilliant Business Blogs, Volume I: The Skills and Techniques You Need* by Suzan St. Maur
- *How to Write Brilliant Business Blogs, Volume II: What to Write About* by Suzan St. Maur
- *The Presentation Book for Senior Managers: An Essential Step by Step Guide to Structuring and Delivering Effective Speeches* by Jay Surti

Announcing the Business Expert Press Digital Library

Concise e-books business students need for classroom and research

This book can also be purchased in an e-book collection by your library as

- a one-time purchase,
- that is owned forever,
- allows for simultaneous readers,
- has no restrictions on printing, and
- can be downloaded as PDFs from within the library community.

Our digital library collections are a great solution to beat the rising cost of textbooks. E-books can be loaded into their course management systems or onto students' e-book readers.
The **Business Expert Press** digital libraries are very affordable, with no obligation to buy in future years. For more information, please visit **www.businessexpertpress.com/librarians**. To set up a trial in the United States, please email **sales@businessexpertpress.com**.

CPSIA information can be obtained
at www.ICGtesting.com
Printed in the USA
FSOW03n2239121117
40933FS